By Milan Blue

Disclaimer:

The information and advice presented in this book are solely for informational purposes. The author and the publisher assume no responsibility for any losses or damages that may arise from the application of the information presented in this book. It is the responsibility of the reader to independently assess and determine whether the content and recommendations presented are suitable for their individual situation. Neither the author nor the publisher are liable for any errors or omissions in this book.

Copyright Disclaimer:

Christian Taormina
c/o IP-Management 30479
Ludwig-Erhard-Str. 18
20459 Hamburg

Basics 7
Patience & Consistency 9
Enjoying Training Sessions 11
Avoiding Punishment 13
Rewards and Treats 15
Training Space 18
Basic Commands 21
Sit 24
Stay 27
Come 30
Drop It 33
Fetch or Retrieve 36
Down 39
Name Recognition 42
Training Fundamental 44
Socialization 45
Alone Time 48
Body Language & Voice Tone 52
Leash & Collar Training 54
Walks 60
Toys 63
Advanced commands 69
Heel 70
Leave It or No 72
Shake 76
Roll Over 80

Specialized Training	82
Crate Training	83
Clicker Training	89
Mental Stimulation	92
Dog sports	97
Jogging	99
Flyball	104
Herding	109
Swimming	113
Rally Obedience	119
Agility	124
Problems	129
Aggression	131
Fear	137
Chewing	142
Nipping	145
Jumping	149
Whining	152
Howling	156
Fleeing	161
Housetraining	165
Barking	168
Professionals	171

Basics

Training a Boxer requires patience, consistency, and a positive mindset. Punishments have no place in effective training; instead, rewards and treats are employed to reinforce desired behaviors. Establishing a conducive training environment, free from distractions, is essential for optimal learning. These foundational principles cultivate a strong bond between Boxer and owner, facilitating the rapid acquisition of new skills. For instance, patience and consistency aid in teaching basic commands like "sit" and "stay," while rewards and treats motivate the repetition of desired behavior. Enjoying the training process enhances the relationship and makes it mutually rewarding.

A Boxer that fails to respond to basic commands such as "sit" or "here" risks venturing onto the street uncontrolled, endangering itself and others by disregarding traffic and acting independently. Practice in various settings to ensure the Boxer can obey commands amidst different distractions. Maintain consistent training methods and always utilize positive reinforcement.

Aggressive behavior towards other dogs can lead to conflicts and tensions, creating unpleasant social dynamics for the Boxer, other dogs, and their owners. To mitigate this risk, consider implementing socialization training to teach the Boxer appropriate interaction with other dogs.

A Boxer that displays disinterest in interacting with its owner and frequently withdraws may indicate a weak bond and low level of trust, resulting in an unsatisfying relationship and frustration for both parties. Investing time in activities such as playing, training, and bonding strengthens the connection between Boxer and owner. This bond transcends training sessions, enriching the overall quality of the owner-Boxer relationship and fostering harmonious coexistence.

Patience & Consistency

Training your Boxer demands a blend of patience, consistency, and thoughtful discipline. Establishing clear expectations, maintaining patience throughout the learning journey, and employing discipline in a fair and constructive manner are paramount.

Patience is paramount in Boxer training. Though intelligent, Boxers may not grasp commands immediately. Embrace patience and empathy as your Boxer assimilates new commands and behaviors. Avoid frustration or anger if your Boxer doesn't succeed initially. Instead, offer gentle guidance, encouragement, and abundant positive reinforcement to aid their progress.

Consistency holds equal importance. Boxers thrive on routine and predictability. Establish and adhere to clear rules and expectations, using consistent commands, gestures, and cues during training. Maintain consistency in praise and rewards for desired behaviors. Inconsistency may confuse and frustrate your Boxer, hindering learning and obedience.

Effective discipline is integral to training but must be wielded judiciously and constructively. Positive re-inforcement, rewarding desired behaviors, is often most effective. However, undesirable behaviors may necessitate correction. Discipline your Boxer calmly and assertively, avoiding physical punishment or aggression. Employ a firm voice and gentle yet firm gestures to convey disapproval, redirecting their attention to more suitable behaviors.

Remember, effective discipline eschews harsh or excessive punishment. Physical reprimands like hitting or yelling can erode trust and potentially incite fear or aggression in your Boxer. Prioritize positive reinforcement and redirection to foster desired behaviors while discouraging unwanted ones.

Enjoying Training Sessions

Training sessions with your Boxer should never feel like a chore; they should be filled with fun and enjoyment. By incorporating games, treats, and ample positive reinforcement, you can transform training into a gratifying and thrilling experience for everyone involved.

Variety is key to keeping training sessions enjoyable for your Boxer. Introduce a mix of exercises and activities to keep them engaged and motivated. Teach new tricks, practice obedience commands in different settings, or introduce agility obstacles for added excitement.

Infuse games into your training sessions to heighten enjoyment for your Boxer. Play fetch, engage in hide and seek, or indulge in a friendly game of tug-of-war to keep them active and stimulated while reinforcing vital skills like recall, focus, and impulse control. Utilize toys, balls, or treats as rewards to maintain motivation and enthusiasm.

Keep training sessions brief and lively to prevent your Boxer from losing interest or becoming frustrated. Aim for sessions lasting no longer than 10-15 minutes at a time, breaking up longer sessions into smaller, more manageable intervals. Conclude each session on a positive note while your Boxer is still eager for more, leaving them excited for the next training opportunity.

Foster a positive and encouraging training environment by maintaining upbeat and enthusiastic energy. Boxers are highly receptive to their owner's emotions, so projecting positivity will help keep them motivated and attentive during training.

Outside of formal training, use play and bonding activities to strengthen your bond with your Boxer. Spend quality time together on walks, engaging in games, or simply sharing cuddles on the couch. Building a foundation of trust and mutual respect will enhance the enjoyment of training sessions.

Remember, learning new skills requires time and repetition, so be patient with your Boxer. Celebrate small victories and progress along the way, and acknowledge their efforts as they strive to master new commands and behaviors.

Avoiding Punishment

Training a Boxer can pose challenges at times, and the temptation to resort to punishment to correct undesired behaviors may arise. However, employing punishment during training can yield a slew of issues and ultimately sabotage your training endeavors.

It's crucial to grasp that punishment-based training methods can erode the bond of trust between you and your Boxer. Boxers are incredibly perceptive animals and may become fearful or anxious in response to harsh or punitive measures. Relying on punishment impedes the establishment of a strong and positive connection.

Furthermore, punishment-based approaches may trigger adverse side effects, including fear, aggression, and avoidance behaviors. Some Boxers may react defensively or aggressively when subjected to punishment, perceiving it as a threat to their well-being. Others may simply learn to avoid certain behaviors altogether, not out of comprehension or obedience, but out of fear of reprisal.

Punishment fails to address the underlying issue behind your Boxer's behavior; it merely suppresses the behavior momentarily. Rather than instructing your Boxer on what to do, punishment merely communicates that they've erred without providing guidance on the correct course of action. This can bewilder and frustrate your Boxer, as they may struggle to comprehend why they're being chastised or how to avoid it in the future.

Instead of punishment, focus on positive re-inforcement to encourage desired behaviors in your Boxer. When they exhibit behaviors you appreciate, such as sitting on command or walking politely on a leash, lavish them with enthusiastic praise and offer treats or toys as rewards. This approach fosters a cooperative and trusting relationship between you and your Boxer, paving the way for successful training outcomes.

Rewards and Treats

One of the most effective ways to motivate and reinforce desired behaviors in your dog is through the use of rewards and treats during training. By offering your dog something they value, such as a tasty treat or a favorite toy, you can encourage them to learn new skills and behaviors while strengthening your bond with them.

By offering rewards for desired behaviors, you can create a positive association with training and motivate your dog to repeat those behaviors in the future.

When choosing treats for training, opt for small, soft, and highly palatable options that your dog can easily chew and swallow. Look for treats that are specifically designed for training purposes, as they are often low in calories and can be broken into small pieces for quick rewards. Experiment with different flavors and textures to find out what your dog likes best and use them as a motivational tool during training sessions.

How do I know which treat my dog likes more?

Recognizing a dog's preferences for certain treats requires keen observation and a sense of their reactions. There are subtle cues that can indicate a dog's preference for a particular treat.

Firstly, it's worth observing the dog's eating behavior. If a dog eagerly devours a treat or chews it with great attention and joy, it suggests that they enjoy it. The speed at which they consume the treat can be an indication of how much they like it.

Another sign of a dog's preference is their search behavior. If they are particularly excited or motivated to get a specific treat, it clearly indicates a strong attraction. A dog that consistently returns to a specific treat when given a choice also shows a clear preference.

Also, observe your dog's physical reactions. Increased salivation or heightened attention when they see or smell the treat can indicate a preference. After consuming a preferred treat, the dog may appear more relaxed or content.

Other Rewards

In addition to treats, you can also use other rewards such as verbal praise, toys, or playtime to reinforce desired behaviors. Dogs respond to a variety of rewards, so mix things up to keep training sessions engaging and exciting for your furry friend.

Timing is crucial when it comes to using rewards and treats in training. It's essential to deliver the reward immediately after your dog performs the desired behavior to reinforce the association between the behavior and the reward.

As you progress with training, gradually reduce the frequency of treats and rewards to encourage your dog to perform behaviors without expecting a reward every time.

Keep training sessions short and focused to prevent your dog from becoming bored or overwhelmed. Aim for sessions lasting no more than 10-15 minutes at a time, and break up longer sessions into smaller, more manageable chunks.

In addition to using rewards and treats during training sessions, incorporate them into your daily interactions with your dog to reinforce good behavior outside of formal training sessions. For example, reward your dog for sitting politely before being fed, or for walking nicely on a leash during walks. By consistently rewarding desired behaviors in various contexts, you can help solidify those behaviors and make them a natural part of your dog's repertoire.

While treats can be highly effective motivators, over-reliance on treats can lead to obesity and other health issues in your dog. Be mindful of the number of treats you're giving your dog and adjust their daily calorie intake accordingly to prevent excessive weight gain.

Training Space

Establishing a dedicated training area for your Boxer is paramount for successful training sessions. Whether you're imparting obedience commands, honing agility skills, or addressing behavioral issues, having a designated space free of distractions is essential.

Select a tranquil and distraction-free locale for your training endeavors. This could be a secluded corner of your living space, a segment of your backyard, or even a serene park or field. The objective is to locate a setting where you and your Boxer can concentrate solely on training without disruptions from noise, passersby, or other animals.

Once you've identified your training space, equip it with all the essential tools and provisions necessary for your sessions. This may entail treats, toys, a leash and collar, as well as training aids or obstacles. Ensuring everything is readily accessible minimizes interruptions and maintains the flow of your training sessions.

Contemplate the layout and arrangement of your training area to optimize learning conditions. Eliminate any potential hazards or impediments that could jeopardize your Boxer's safety, such as sharp objects, electrical cords, or toxic flora. Maintain cleanliness and organization to foster a secure and inviting atmosphere conducive to learning and play.

Establish boundaries or barriers to delineate the training zone and prevent your Boxer from straying or becoming distracted. Employ baby gates, exercise pens, or visual markers like cones or flags to demarcate clear boundaries, fostering your Boxer's focus on the designated tasks.

Consider the lighting and ambient temperature of your training space to ensure your Boxer's comfort and well-being. Opt for a well-illuminated area with ample natural light or supplement with artificial lighting for indoor sessions. This is particularly crucial if training outdoors in extreme weather conditions.

Facilitate ample opportunities for your Boxer to rest and rejuvenate during training sessions. Arrange a cozy mat or bed where your Boxer can unwind between exercises and take breaks as necessary. Encourage relaxation with soothing praise or gentle caresses, permitting your Boxer to replenish their energy reserves for subsequent training endeavors.

Basic Commands

Training a Boxer in basic commands is a fundamental aspect of responsible pet ownership, offering numerous benefits for both the Boxer and their owner. These foundational commands lay the groundwork for effective communication and collaboration between the Boxer and their owner.

Moreover, basic command training provides mental stimulation and engagement for the Boxer. Short, regular training sessions offer opportunities for Boxers to exercise their cognitive faculties, enhancing focus, attention, and problem-solving abilities. This mental stimulation is crucial for warding off boredom and addressing behavioral issues such as destructive chewing or excessive barking, by redirecting the Boxer's energy into positive activities.

Regarding the duration required to train a Boxer in basic commands through 10-minute daily sessions, the timeframe may vary. Generally, with consistent practice and positive reinforcement, many Boxers can grasp basic commands within a few weeks to a month. However, individual progress may differ, with some Boxers mastering concepts more swiftly than others. The key lies in maintaining patience, consistency, and support throughout the training journey, progressively advancing upon each command as the Boxer grows more adept.

Before commencing a training session, ensure you are in a tranquil environment, such as at home without distractions. It's crucial to gradually introduce environmental changes to challenge the Boxer. For instance, transition to the garden where they may encounter bird sounds or sights, but only after successfully executing commands multiple times without issues. Once proficient in the garden setting, expose the Boxer to further challenges, such as training in a park amidst other dogs, people, or noises.

Possible distractions during training could include:
- Other pets nearby, such as cats or other dogs that may be playing or barking.
- Passing individuals or neighbors engaging in conversations or creating noise.
- Street noises like cars, bicycles, or traffic sounds.
- Playing children nearby.
- Birds or other animals in the garden or park.
- Movements or sounds from objects like wind, fluttering flags, or falling leaves.
- Changing weather conditions like rain, wind, or sunshine.
- Smells of food or other animals in the vicinity.
- Unfamiliar objects or situations that might pique the dog's curiosity.

In the past, dogs had to hunt for their food, which was a natural challenge that boosted their motivation. Hungry dogs are usually more eager to do tasks because they're driven by their need for food. A good idea for dog owners might be to train their dogs before feeding them. They could even skip a meal to make the training more intense.

A full stomach might make dogs less willing to make an effort. So, taking a walk or doing training before feeding could be the best time to use the dog's energy and focus.

But it's important to make sure the dog isn't hungry just to be motivated. This approach should be seen as a way to use the dog's natural motivation without harming its well-being. Also, it's important not to overdo tasty treats, as they also count as food for the dog. Otherwise, the dog might get full and then not want to eat its proper meal.

Dogs require 20-30 repetitions after each small step to truly learn and master commands during training. It's important to be patient and give them enough time to internalize each step. This means that regular practice sessions and repetitions are essential to solidify their skills.

When it comes to rewarding in training, it's important to pay attention to how it's used. Instead of rewarding the dog when it makes a mistake, the reward should come when it moves in the right direction or performs the desired behavior correctly. This way, the dog learns what is expected of it, and its training successes will be more effective.

Before starting the training, it's important to have treats ready at hand. When you begin teaching commands, call your dog's name to get their attention. This ensures you have a successful training session.

In the upcoming chapters, we'll break down the following commands step by step for easier understanding.

Sit

The "sit" command holds particular significance as it often serves as the foundational command in a dog's training journey. It's typically the first command taught to a dog, establishing the groundwork for further obedience training. This foundational aspect underscores its importance, as mastering the "sit" command lays the groundwork for teaching more complex behaviors and commands.

Moreover, the "sit" command is useful for controlling the dog in various situations, such as during leash walking, crossing streets, or greeting guests. A dog that has mastered the "sit" command is easier to control and can respond more quickly to commands.

Additionally, the "sit" command can be helpful for interrupting undesirable behavior. By teaching the dog to respond to the "sit" command, the owner can distract them and divert them from potentially dangerous or problematic situations.

The utility of the "sit" command extends to situations within the household as well. For instance, it can assist in keeping the dog calm when guests enter the house or when family members are eating. A dog that masters the "sit" command is less likely to beg for food intrusively and will instead remain composed. Additionally, during vet visits or grooming tasks such as brushing or trimming nails, the "sit" command can be extremely helpful as it allows the dog to remain calm and cooperative.

Here's a step-by-step guide on how to teach it:
- Grab your dog's attention by calling their name in an upbeat tone. Once you have their focus, hold a treat in

your hand, allowing them to see and smell it. This will pique their interest and motivate them to engage in the training.

- With the treat in hand, position it close to your dog's nose and slowly move it upwards and slightly backward over their head. As your dog follows the movement of the treat, their natural response will be to lift their head and sit down.
- The moment your dog's bottom touches the ground, say the command "sit" in a clear and firm voice. Timing is crucial here – it's essential to utter the command at the exact moment your dog assumes the sitting position. This helps them associate the word with the action.
- Immediately after your dog sits, praise them enthusiastically and give them the treat as a reward. Positive reinforcement is key to reinforcing desired behaviors. Repeat this sequence several times, each time using the treat to lure your dog into the sitting position and rewarding them when they comply.
- Once your dog starts to understand the command and consistently sits on cue, you can begin to phase out the treat lure gradually. Instead of holding the treat in your hand, use an empty hand gesture to guide your dog into

the sitting position. Remember to still reward them with verbal praise and occasional treats for their efforts.

Should I physically help my dog to sit if he doesn't obey the command immediately?
It's important for your dog to learn and respond to the "sit" command, but physical assistance should only be used as a last resort. This should be avoided as it can create confusion towards you as the owner.

Can I use the "sit" command to correct certain behavioral problems in my dog, such as begging for food?
The "sit" command can be an effective tool to address certain behavioral issues in dogs, including begging for food. Teaching your dog to sit on command can redirect their attention from unwanted behaviors like begging for food.

Here's how you could proceed: When your dog begs, you could kindly but firmly ask him to sit. Once he does, immediately reward him with praise, a treat, or a toy. This way, your dog associates sitting with positive experiences and learns that this behavior is rewarded.

However, it's important to note that the "sit" command alone may not be sufficient to permanently correct begging behavior. It's advisable to also employ other techniques of behavior modification. This includes, for example, ignoring the unwanted behavior and instead rewarding alternative behavior, such as calmly lying down or playing with a toy.

It's also important to ensure that all family members and visitors are consistent and do not inadvertently reinforce begging behavior by giving the dog food when he begs.

Stay

The command "Stay" is crucial for ensuring the safety of your dog. A dog that masters this command remains securely in place even in public areas such as parks or cafes, without rushing towards other people or animals.

Examples of applying the "Stay" command could include:
- When opening the front door, you can give your dog the command "Stay" to prevent it from running outside.
- While taking a walk, you can teach your dog to stay in a specific spot while allowing it to relax and explore the surroundings.
- When receiving guests, the "Stay" command can help your dog remain calm and controlled instead of jumping around excitedly or barking.
- During a visit to the vet, you can encourage your dog to stay in its place while you speak with the vet or wait for treatment.

Here are some things to avoid when using the "Stay" command:
- Sudden Departures: Avoid suddenly and unexpectedly moving away from your dog while practicing the "Stay" command. This can confuse your dog and lead to a lack of trust in the command.
- Excessive Distances: Do not start with too great a distance when trying to get your dog to stay in place. Begin with short distances and gradually increase them as your dog better understands the command and becomes more obedient.

- Excessive Waiting: Do not push your dog beyond its abilities by holding it in the "Stay" position for too long. Start with short time intervals and gradually increase them to improve your dog's ability to follow the command.

Here's a step-by-step guide on how to teach it:

- Begin by commanding your dog to sit. This sets the foundation for the "stay" command, as your dog needs to be in a stationary position initially. Once your dog is seated, offer praise and a treat to reinforce the behavior.
- With your dog in the sitting position, extend your hand, palm facing towards your dog, and say the command "stay" in a clear and firm voice. The hand signal serves as a visual cue to accompany the verbal command and helps reinforce understanding.
- After giving the command, take a small step backward away from your dog. Maintain eye contact and encourage them to stay in place using a calm and reassuring tone. If your dog remains seated, offer praise and a treat as a reward.
- Once your dog is comfortable with you stepping back, gradually increase the distance between you and your dog. Take a few more steps backward while continuing to maintain eye contact and reinforcing the "stay" command.

- As your dog becomes more proficient, begin to increase the duration of the stay. Start with short intervals and gradually extend the time your dog is required to remain in place before receiving the release command.
- After a successful stay, release your dog from the command by using a release cue such as "okay" or "free." Offer praise and a treat to reward your dog for their obedience. It's essential to make the release cue distinct from the stay command to avoid confusion.
- If your dog struggles with the "stay" command, go back to previous steps and reinforce the basics before progressing further. Break down the training into smaller, manageable steps, and be patient with your dog's progress.

Come

The "Come" command is a fundamentally important tool in dog training, crucial in numerous everyday situations.

During a walk, a dog might become excited or distracted and wander off. In such moments, the "Come" command is crucial to safely recall the dog, especially if it's in danger, such as near a busy road.

Encounters with other dogs or people require a dog to listen to its owner's signal and return to them. This not only enables control over the situation but also fosters positive socialization and prevents potential conflicts.

Even in enclosed areas like the house or garden, the "Come" command is significant. For example, if a door is accidentally left open or the dog is unsupervised outside, a quick and reliable recall ensures the dog doesn't escape or get into dangerous situations.

The "Come" command is also a fundamental element in obedience training. Through regular practice and rewarding, the dog learns that coming back to its owner is positively reinforced, leading to reliable obedience.

In emergencies such as injuries or sudden threats, the "Come" command can be lifesaving. It allows the owner to quickly regain control of the dog and lead it away from potentially dangerous situations.

Here's a step-by-step guide on how to teach it:
- With your dog's attention on you, give the command "come" in a clear and inviting tone. Use a hand gesture, such as patting your leg or extending your arm, to further encourage your dog to approach you.
- As soon as your dog starts moving towards you, offer praise and encouragement. When they reach you, reward

them with a treat and plenty of verbal praise. Positive reinforcement helps your dog associate the action of coming when called with a pleasant reward.

- Once your dog understands the concept of coming when called, gradually increase the distance between you and your dog. Start with short distances and gradually extend the range as your dog becomes more proficient.
- Practice the "come" command in different environments and situations to generalize the behavior. Start in familiar settings and gradually introduce distractions, such as other people, animals, or noises. This helps your dog learn to respond reliably regardless of the surroundings.
- During the training process, you may need to use the leash to guide your dog towards you if they hesitate or become distracted. However, avoid pulling or yanking on the leash, as this can create a negative association with the command.
- If your dog doesn't come when called, avoid scolding or punishing them. Instead, go back to earlier steps and reinforce the behavior with positive reinforcement. Punishment can undermine your dog's trust and willingness to obey.
- Incorporate recall games into your training routine to make learning fun and engaging for your dog. Play games such as hide-and-seek or chase, where you call your dog to

come and reward them with treats or toys when they find you.

What should be avoided to prevent misunderstandings or problems when using the 'come' command?
To avoid misunderstandings or problems when using the "come" command, it's important not to overuse it, as this can lead to the dog ignoring the signal or considering it irrelevant. Instead, the command should only be applied in situations where an immediate return of the dog is necessary.

Drop It

The command "Drop it" is a crucial element in training a dog, as it teaches the dog to release objects it has in its mouth on command. This command is essential for several reasons.

Firstly, it concerns the safety of the dog. In many cases, a dog may inadvertently ingest dangerous or unwanted objects, whether it's a piece of chocolate that's toxic to them or a sharp object that can cause injury. By promptly obeying the "Drop it" command, the dog can immediately release such potentially harmful items, minimizing potential health risks and even being life-saving.

Secondly, the "Drop it" command is an important part of obedience training. An obedient dog trained to respond to its owner's commands is safer and more enjoyable to be around. For example, if the dog picks up an object outdoors that it shouldn't keep, an immediate "Drop it" command can lead the dog to release the item and return it to the owner.

Thirdly, the "Drop it" command enables smooth play and safe interaction between the dog and its owner. In activities such as retrieving or interactive toy play, it's important for the dog to be able to release the object on command so that the game can continue. A dog that masters the "Drop it" command can playfully interact with its owner without conflicts or issues arising.

Here's a step-by-step guide on how to teach it:
- Before diving into training, ensure that you have established a trusting relationship. This foundation of trust will make the training process smoother and more effective.

- Begin by engaging your dog in play with a favorite toy. Allow them to hold the toy in their mouth and play tug-of-war if they enjoy it. This step helps create a natural scenario for practicing the "drop it" command.
- Once your dog has a firm grip on the toy, show them a tempting treat or another toy of equal or higher value. Use it to lure your dog's attention away from the original toy they're holding.
- As you present the trade item, say the command "drop it" in a clear and firm tone. It's essential to use a consistent verbal cue so your dog can associate the command with the action of releasing the object from their mouth.
- The moment your dog releases the toy from their mouth, immediately praise them and offer the trade item as a reward. Positive reinforcement helps your dog understand that complying with the "drop it" command leads to a positive outcome.
- Repeat the exercise multiple times, gradually reducing the lure of the trade item until your dog responds reliably to the verbal command alone. Practice in short, frequent sessions to reinforce the behavior and build consistency.
- Once your dog understands the "drop it" command with toys, generalize the behavior to other objects they may encounter, such as household items or items found during walks. Practice in various settings to ensure your dog responds consistently in different situations.
- Always prioritize your dog's safety during training. If your dog refuses to drop a potentially harmful object, never force it out of their mouth.

When using the "Drop it" command, there are some important things to consider to ensure that the training is effective and does not reinforce unwanted behaviors:

Avoid forced removal: Refrain from forcibly removing an object from the dog's mouth, especially if the dog tends to resource guard. This can lead to aggression and undermine the dog's trust in you. The "Drop it" command is intended to teach the dog to voluntarily release objects without coercion.

Avoid overuse: Try not to use the "Drop it" command too frequently and in situations where the dog doesn't necessarily need it. This could diminish the effectiveness of the command or cause the dog to ignore it. Reserve the command for situations where it's genuinely important for the dog to release an object.

Avoid building pressure: Refrain from pressuring or harassing the dog if it doesn't immediately release an object. Patience is crucial, and it may take some time for the dog to reliably execute the command. Coercion can lead to stress and hinder the dog's learning process.

Fetch or Retrieve

Fetching or retrieving items is important for dogs for several reasons.

Secondly, fetching is a form of physical exercise and training. When a dog runs to fetch a ball or a toy and brings it back, they are exercising their muscles and improving their endurance. This is particularly important for dogs with high energy levels that require regular exercise to stay healthy.

Here is a list of situations and places where you can use the commands "Fetch" and "Retrieve":
- During a walk in the park, the owner can encourage the dog to fetch and retrieve a ball or a toy to provide mental stimulation and physical exercise.
- In their own garden, owners can play and train with their dogs by prompting them to fetch and retrieve items such as frisbees or toys.
- Indoors, the commands "Fetch" and "Retrieve" can also be useful for getting the dog to bring back items they have found or that the owner needs, such as slippers or toys.
- For dogs recovering from injuries or surgeries, fetching items can be a gentle form of physical rehabilitation that helps restore their mobility and muscle strength.

Here's a step-by-step guide on how to teach it:
- Start by selecting a suitable toy for fetching, such as a tennis ball, a plush toy, or a frisbee. Choose a toy that is easy for your dog to pick up and carry in their mouth. Additionally, ensure that the toy is safe and durable for interactive play.

- Before introducing the fetch command, get your dog excited about the toy by encouraging them to play with it. Toss the toy gently in front of them and encourage them to pick it up. Use enthusiastic praise and encouragement to make the toy seem irresistible to your dog.
- Once your dog is engaged with the toy, introduce the fetch command by saying "fetch" in a clear and enthusiastic tone. Use a hand gesture, such as pointing towards the toy, to further reinforce the command visually.
- Encourage your dog to retrieve the toy by pointing towards it and using an excited tone of voice. If necessary, take a few steps towards the toy to demonstrate what you want your dog to do.
- When your dog picks up the toy and brings it back to you, reward them with praise and a treat. Positive reinforcement helps your dog associate fetching with a positive outcome, making them more eager to repeat the behavior.
- As your dog becomes more proficient at fetching, gradually increase the distance between you and the toy. Start by tossing the toy a short distance away and gradually increase the distance as your dog's skills improve.
- Introduce challenges to make fetching more engaging and mentally stimulating for your dog. You can hide the toy behind obstacles or toss it into tall grass for your dog to search and retrieve.
- To keep your dog interested in fetching, vary the toys you use and rotate them regularly. Some dogs may prefer certain types of toys over others, so experiment to find what motivates your dog the most.
- Most importantly, have fun playing fetch with your dog! Enjoy the bonding experience and celebrate your dog's achievements as they master the art of fetching.

What is the difference between Fetch and Retrieve?
The difference between Fetch and Retrieve lies in the context and terminology. "Fetch" generally refers to the action of the dog bringing back an object that its owner has thrown. It's a command for the dog to search for, seize, and return the object. "Retrieve" can be used as a more general term referring to the action of bringing back an object, whether it was thrown or not. However, in many cases, the terms are used interchangeably to describe the same behavior.

What risks arise when training "Fetch" and "Retrieve" excessively?
Excessive emphasis on Fetch and Retrieve could lead to the dog becoming fixated on these activities, potentially resulting in frustration or boredom if unable to perform these behaviors. This could lead to undesirable behaviors such as excessive barking, object destruction, or even aggression.

Down

The command 'down' is an essential element in a dog's training as it teaches them to lie down and behave calmly. In everyday life, the 'down' command can be used in various situations, including:

- When the dog needs to remain calm while visitors are in the house.
- During visits to the veterinarian to calm the dog and facilitate examination.
- While eating to prevent the dog from begging for food.
- When the dog is too excited and needs to be calmed down.
- In situations where the dog is excessively staring at or barking at other animals or people, to calm and control them.

Here's a step-by-step guide on how to teach it:

- Begin by commanding your dog to sit. This sets the foundation for the "down" command, as your dog needs to be in a seated position initially. Once your dog is seated, offer praise and a treat to reinforce the behavior.
- With a treat in your hand, hold it close to your dog's nose and slowly lower it towards the ground. As your dog

follows the movement of the treat, their natural response will be to lower their body towards the ground.

- The moment your dog's chest and elbows touch the ground, say the command "down" in a clear and firm voice. Timing is crucial here – it's essential to utter the command at the exact moment your dog assumes the lying down position.
- Immediately after your dog lies down, praise them enthusiastically and give them the treat as a reward. Positive reinforcement is key to reinforcing desired behaviors. Repeat this sequence several times, using the treat to lure your dog into the lying down position and rewarding them when they comply.
- Once your dog starts to understand the command and consistently lies down on cue, you can begin to phase out the treat lure gradually. Instead of holding the treat in your hand, use an empty hand gesture to guide your dog into the lying down position. Remember to still reward them with verbal praise and occasional treats for their efforts.
- Practice the "down" command with your dog daily, gradually increasing the level of difficulty by introducing distractions or practicing in different locations. Be patient and understanding, as every dog learns at their own pace.
- Even after your dog has mastered the "down" command, it's essential to continue reinforcing it regularly to maintain their obedience. Use the command in daily interactions and reward your dog for complying, ensuring that they remain responsive and attentive.

If your dog lies down but immediately gets back up, it could have various reasons. Here are some tips on how to correct this behavior:

Gradually increase the duration: Start by teaching your dog to lie down for a short period and then reward them. Gradually increase the time they should remain in the lying position before rewarding them. This way, your dog learns that they need to lie down longer to receive the reward.

Use a release word: Use a release word like 'Okay' or 'Free' to signal to your dog that they can get up. By using a release word, your dog learns to get up only when you give them the signal.

Use distractions: To help your dog stay lying down longer, you can engage them with distractions such as a toy or treat that they only receive after lying down for a certain time."

Name Recognition

Name recognition in dogs is important because it forms the foundation for effective communication between the dog and its owner. When a dog knows and responds to its name, it greatly facilitates interaction and training.

By recognizing its name, a dog can better respond to commands and follow instructions. This is particularly important in situations where safety and control are necessary, such as walking in public places or training for obedience.

Here's a step-by-step guide on how to teach it to your dog:

- Start by saying your dog's name in a clear and upbeat tone. Use a tone of voice that is distinct from your everyday speech to capture your dog's attention effectively. When your dog looks at you upon hearing their name, immediately reward them with praise or a treat.
- Practice name recognition exercises regularly throughout the day, gradually increasing the level of difficulty. Start in a quiet environment with minimal distractions and gradually progress to more challenging situations, such as when your dog is engaged in play or exploring their surroundings.
- Once your dog reliably responds to their name in close proximity, gradually increase the distance between you and your dog. Practice calling their name from across the room or yard, rewarding them when they respond by looking at you.
- Make name recognition training fun and engaging by incorporating name games into your routine. For example, scatter treats or toys around the room and call your dog's

name to encourage them to search for and retrieve the items. This not only reinforces name recognition but also provides mental stimulation for your dog.

What you should never do:

Punishment: Never punish your dog for not responding to their name. Negative reinforcement can make your dog fearful or insecure and can damage the trust between you and your dog.

Excessive Repetition: Avoid excessive repetition of your dog's name, as this can lead to them ignoring it. If your dog doesn't respond to their name, try to get their attention in other ways before using their name again.

Using the Name in Negative Contexts: Avoid using your dog's name in connection with negative events or punishments. This can cause your dog to associate their name with negative experiences and be less likely to respond to it.

Training Fundamental

After mastering the basic commands and training principles, it's time to focus on the foundations of dog training. In this section, we will delve deeper into the topics of socialization, alone training, body language, tone of voice, leash and collar training, walks, and toys. These elements form the backbone of successful dog training and contribute to building a deep bond between you and your dog. Let's dive into these fascinating aspects together and lay the groundwork for a happy and fulfilling human-dog relationship.

Socialization

It's crucial to assist your Boxer in feeling comfortable and confident in various social settings, encompassing interactions with other dogs, people, and new environments.

Socialization commences at a young age and persists throughout your Boxer's life. Early socialization, particularly during the critical period between 3 and 14 weeks of age, is paramount when puppies are most open to new encounters and impressions. During this phase, expose your puppy to diverse sights, sounds, scents, and sensations to foster positive associations and diminish the likelihood of fear or anxiety in the future.

Introduce your puppy to a spectrum of individuals encompassing all ages, genders, and ethnicities, as well as other animals such as dogs, cats, and small creatures.

Expose your puppy to an array of settings and stimuli, spanning various surfaces, textures, and environments like parks, streets, and indoor areas. Gradually introduce them to novel experiences and scenarios at their own pace, offering patience and support as they navigate unfamiliar terrain. Utilize positive reinforcement techniques to instill confidence and security in new environments, and be prepared to pause or retreat if they become overwhelmed.

As your puppy matures, continue prioritizing socialization and exposure to fresh encounters. Regularly expose them to diverse people, locales, and circumstances to uphold their social aptitude and adaptability.

Understand that socialization extends beyond mere exposure to novel experiences; it's also about teaching your dog appropriate behavior in diverse situations. Establish clear boundaries and expectations for your Boxer's conduct, ensuring they interact politely and respectfully with individuals and fellow animals.

Proactively address any fears or anxieties your Boxer may harbor concerning new experiences or situations. If your Boxer exhibits signs of fear or discomfort, such as trembling, cowering, or attempting to flee, avoid forcing them to confront their fears. Instead, provide reassurance and encouragement, gradually introducing them to the trigger at a slower pace or from a greater distance until they feel at ease.

In addition to exposing your Boxer to new encounters, facilitate ample opportunities for positive social interactions and playtime with fellow dogs. Boxers are innately social beings and benefit from regular chances to engage and socialize with their canine counterparts. Arrange playdates with friends or family members who own dogs, or enroll your Boxer in group training sessions or doggy daycare programs to nurture their social skills in a supervised and controlled setting.

Socialization with Dogs and Other Animals

Whether it's mingling with fellow canines at the park, exchanging greetings with a neighbor's cat, or encountering wildlife during a hike, exposure to diverse animals aids in fostering crucial social skills in dogs and teaches them how to communicate and coexist harmoniously with other creatures.

Introduce your Boxer to other dogs gradually and serenely, permitting them to sniff and greet one another at their own pace. Refrain from compelling interactions or inundating your Boxer with too many unfamiliar dogs simultaneously, as this may induce stress or anxiety. Instead, concentrate on cultivating positive encounters and reinforcing desirable behavior with praise and treats.

Beyond socializing with other dogs, it's equally imperative for Boxers to interact with alternative animals like cats, rabbits, and small mammals. These interactions aid Boxers in learning appropriate conduct around diverse species and can avert fear or aggression towards unfamiliar animals in the future.

When acquainting your Boxer with other animals, prioritize safety and supervision at all times. Secure smaller animals in a crate or on a leash, and closely oversee their interactions with your Boxer.

Initiating socialization with other animals from a young age is vital, but it's never too late to commence. Even adult Boxers can derive benefits from exposure to new animals and environments, although they may necessitate a slower and more gradual approach to socialization.

Alone Time

Leaving your cherished Boxer alone for prolonged periods can result in a range of adverse effects, from boredom to potential behavioral issues. Each Boxer is unique, with individual needs and preferences influenced by factors such as age, breed, temperament, and personality. It's crucial to acknowledge these factors when determining how long a Boxer can comfortably be left alone.

Particularly with puppies, it's essential to recognize that their small bladders and limited attention spans necessitate more frequent breaks and attention compared to adult dogs. These tender souls require extra love and care to prevent feelings of loneliness or anxiety when left unaccompanied.

While there's a general guideline suggesting that most adult Boxers can tolerate being left alone for about four to eight hours, this estimate isn't rigid. Some Boxers may manage longer periods solo, while others may exhibit signs of distress or unease after a shorter duration.

Several factors influence the duration a Boxer can be left alone, including their activity level and overall health. Apart from fulfilling their basic needs for sustenance and hydration, it's essential to provide mental and physical stimulation to keep them engaged and content during your absence. Offering a variety of toys, puzzles, and enrichment activities can help engage their minds and stave off boredom.

If you anticipate leaving your Boxer alone for an extended period, consider seeking assistance from friends, family members, or professional pet sitters to ensure they receive companionship and care in your absence. Alternatively, you may opt for doggy daycare services or hire a dog walker to provide them with exercise and social interaction.

How can I tell if my dog is suffering from separation anxiety?

Separation anxiety is a common issue in dogs and can manifest in various behaviors. It's important to recognize the signs of separation anxiety in order to intervene in a timely manner and improve your dog's well-being.

Signs of separation anxiety:
- Excessive barking, howling, or whining, especially shortly after the owner leaves the house.
- Destruction of items in the house, such as furniture or shoes.
- Inappropriate elimination, such as urinating or defecating in the house, even though the dog is normally house-trained.
- Signs of stress, such as excessive panting, trembling, or drooling.

Keep a diary of your dog's behavior when you leave the house to identify patterns and determine if he is showing signs of separation anxiety. The earlier you recognize the signs, the sooner you can take appropriate action.

Measures to adjust your dog's environment:
- Allow your dog to stay in a room or area where he feels comfortable and safe, with access to his favorite spots and items.
- Provide toys, chew treats, or interactive puzzles to keep your dog occupied and entertained during your absence.
- Say goodbye calmly and quietly to your dog, avoiding excessive emotional reactions to avoid exacerbating his anxiety.

- Create a calm and relaxed environment for your dog by playing soothing music or providing access to a cozy sleeping area.
- Ensure that your dog's environment is safe and free from potential hazards such as toxic plants or choking hazards.

Experiment with various adjustments in your dog's environment and observe how he responds. Every dog is unique, so it may take some time to find the best environment to reduce his anxiety and improve his well-being.

To successfully manage your dog's separation anxiety, it's important to understand deeper aspects of dealing with this issue and avoid certain behaviors that can exacerbate your dog's anxiety.

An excessive farewell ceremony, such as lengthy goodbyes, hugs, or tears, may signal to your dog that your absence is something to worry about. This can amplify his separation anxiety by conveying the message that your absence is a cause for concern. Similarly, you should not punish your dog when you come home and notice behavioral problems, such as destruction or soiling. Punishment upon return will not associate your dog's behavior during your absence and may exacerbate his anxiety as he associates your negative reaction with your return.

Irregular absences should be avoided as they can be unpredictable and stressful for your dog, which can exacerbate his separation anxiety. It's important to make your absence times as consistent as possible to provide your dog with a sense of security and predictability.

The importance of adequate physical and mental stimulation for your dog should not be overlooked. Boredom and under-stimulation can exacerbate separation anxiety. Therefore, it's important to provide your dog with enough activities and engagement to mentally and physically exhaust him. Do not neglect preparing your dog for alone time. Do not leave him unprepared alone, especially if he suffers from separation anxiety. Gradually prepare him for alone time and ensure he has the necessary resources to feel comfortable and safe.

By avoiding these behaviors and instead taking positive and supportive measures, you can help reduce your dog's separation anxiety and provide him with a happier and more balanced life.

Body Language & Voice Tone

When it comes to communication, every dog breed has its own way of expressing themselves. The Boxer dog is no exception. With their expressive faces and playful demeanor, Boxers have a distinct body language and voice tone that sets them apart from other breeds.

Body Language

Boxers are known for their animated facial expressions and lively body movements. One of the most recognizable features of a Boxer is their "wiggle butt" – a unique wiggling motion of their rear end when they're excited or happy. This wagging is often accompanied by a big, toothy grin that stretches from ear to ear, showcasing their friendly and outgoing nature.

When a Boxer is feeling relaxed and content, you may notice them lying on their back with their legs in the air, inviting belly rubs. This vulnerable position is a sign of trust and affection towards their human companions. However, if a Boxer feels threatened or uncomfortable, they may exhibit defensive behaviors such as standing stiffly, raising their hackles, or curling their lips into a snarl.

Boxers are also notorious for their "Boxer lean" – a habit of leaning their body weight against their favorite humans or objects. This behavior is a sign of affection and a way for Boxers to feel close and connected to their loved ones.

Voice Tone

While Boxers are not typically known for being excessive barkers, they are not afraid to use their voice to communicate. Boxers have a unique vocalization known as the "woo-woo," which is a combination of a bark and a whine. This distinctive sound is often used to express excitement, anticipation, or a desire for attention.

In addition to their vocalizations, Boxers are highly attuned to human voice tones and body language. They are incredibly responsive to positive reinforcement training methods and thrive on praise and encouragement from their owners. A cheerful and upbeat tone of voice is most effective when training a Boxer, as it motivates them to learn and perform tasks eagerly.

However, Boxers can also pick up on subtle changes in tone and mood. If their owner sounds stern or disappointed, a Boxer may become subdued or apologetic, eager to please and make amends. Conversely, a happy and enthusiastic tone will elicit wagging tails and excited jumps, as Boxers feed off the energy and emotions of those around them.

Leash & Collar Training

Leashes and collars are more than just accessories for your dog; they're tools that help you communicate and keep your dog safe during walks.

Leashes come in various shapes, sizes, and

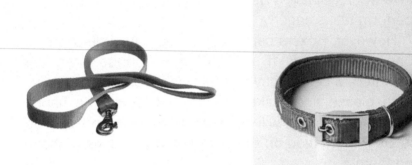

materials, but their primary purpose is to keep your dog under control while you're out and about. Whether it's a standard nylon leash, a retractable leash, or a sturdy leather leash, the key is to choose one that suits your dog's size, strength, and behavior.

The leash attaches to your dog's collar or harness, allowing you to guide and direct them as you walk together. Collars come in different styles too, from traditional buckle collars to martingale collars and harnesses. Each serves a specific purpose, whether it's for training, control, or safety.

When using a collar, it's essential to ensure that it fits properly and comfortably around your dog's neck. You should be able to fit two fingers between the collar and your dog's neck to ensure a snug but not too tight fit. This prevents the collar from slipping off or causing discomfort to your dog.

If your dog tends to pull or lunge during walks, a harness might be a better option. Harnesses distribute pressure more evenly across your dog's body, reducing the risk of injury and providing better control. Look for a harness with adjustable straps and padding for maximum comfort.

Teaching acceptance of the leash and collar

For many dogs, wearing a leash and collar can feel strange and uncomfortable at first. You can teach your dog to accept and even enjoy wearing them.

Start by introducing your dog to the leash and collar in a calm and relaxed environment. Let them sniff and explore the new accessories at their own pace, using treats and praise to create a positive association. Gradually introduce the leash and collar, allowing your dog to wear them for short periods indoors before venturing outside.

When putting on the leash and collar, use gentle and reassuring movements to avoid startling your dog. If your dog shows signs of discomfort or resistance, take a step back and give them time to adjust before trying again.

Once your dog is comfortable wearing the leash and collar indoors, it's time to venture outside for short walks. Start in a familiar and low-stress environment, like your backyard or a quiet neighborhood street. Keep the walks short and relaxed, allowing your dog to explore and adjust to the sights and sounds of the outdoors.

During walks, pay attention to your dog's body language and behavior. If they seem anxious or stressed, take a break and offer reassurance before continuing.

As your dog becomes more comfortable with wearing the leash and collar, gradually increase the duration and intensity of your walks. Explore new environments and experiences together, allowing your dog to build confidence and trust in you as their guide.

Training not to pull on the leash and collar

One of the most common challenges dog owners face during walks is dealing with a dog that pulls on the leash. It can be frustrating and even dangerous if your dog lunges or drags you along.

First, it's essential to understand why dogs pull on the leash. Dogs are naturally curious creatures, and they're eager to explore their surroundings. When they see something interesting or exciting, like a squirrel or another dog, they may instinctively pull towards it. Additionally, if they haven't been taught proper leash manners, they may simply be unaware of how to walk politely.

The good news is that you can teach your dog not to pull on the leash through positive reinforcement training. The key is to reward desired behavior, such as walking calmly beside you, and to redirect or ignore unwanted behavior, such as pulling or lunging.

Here's a guide for leash training when your dog pulls during walks:

If your dog starts pulling on the leash, immediately stop and stand still. Avoid stopping your dog by pulling on the leash, as this can signal to them that pulling is rewarded.

Loosen the leash so there is no tension on it. You could also walk in the opposite direction to show your dog that pulling does not lead to the desired outcome.
Wait patiently until your dog relaxes and the leash loosens. It may take a while for your dog to understand what you want from them.

Once your dog relaxes and the leash loosens, reward them immediately with praise and treats.

When your dog has calmed down and the leash is loose, continue the walk. Make sure to give your dog enough space to move without having to pull on the leash.

Repeat these steps consistently every time your dog pulls on the leash. Over time, your dog will learn that pulling is not rewarded and that it's worth staying relaxed by your side.

Another helpful technique is to use a front-clip harness or head halter. These tools provide more control and can help discourage pulling by gently steering your dog back towards you when they start to pull. However, it's essential to use these tools properly and humanely, and to continue training your dog to walk politely on a loose leash.

Avoid using punishment or harsh corrections when training your dog not to pull on the leash. This can cause stress and confusion for your dog and may even worsen the problem. Celebrate the small victories along the way, and don't be discouraged by setbacks.

Why does my dog bite the leash?

If a dog bites at its leash, it can be attributed to various causes. A common reason is boredom or excess energy. Dogs that do not receive enough exercise or mental stimulation may feel bored and try to expend their energy by pulling or biting on the leash. This can especially occur when the dog is kept indoors for extended periods or lacks sufficient opportunities to play and explore.

Another factor could be stress or anxiety. Dogs may bite at their leash when they are in stressful or frightening situations, such as loud noises, unfamiliar environments, or encounters with other dogs or people that intimidate them. Biting on the leash can be a coping mechanism to deal with these feelings or to defend themselves.

A lack of understanding of leash manners can also lead to this behavior. If a dog has not been properly trained to walk on a leash, it may start pulling or biting out of frustration or confusion. In some cases, the dog may be attempting to take control because it has not learned that the human takes the lead and sets the direction.

Additionally, excitement can also play a role. Some dogs may bite at their leash when they are excited, whether it's anticipation of a walk, meeting other dogs, or simply due to stimuli in their environment. In such moments, biting on the leash can be a way to discharge these emotions.

It's important to carefully observe your dog's behavior and identify potential triggers. Through consistent training and positive reinforcement, you can teach your dog to exhibit appropriate leash behavior. If you're having difficulty solving the problem on your own, the assistance of a professional dog trainer or behavior consultant may be helpful in identifying the cause of the behavior and finding appropriate solutions.

Tips

Stay calm: Remain calm and composed even if your dog bites on the leash. Stand still calmly and avoid pulling on the leash to prevent reinforcing any negative reactions from your dog.

Interrupt the behavior: Once your dog starts biting on the leash, interrupt the behavior with a clear "No!" or another marker word you use for undesirable behavior. Avoid loud shouts or sudden movements that might startle your dog.

Provide distraction: Redirect your dog's attention away from the leash by offering a toy or a treat. Distract them to lose interest in the leash and focus on something positive instead.

Timing of reward: As soon as your dog stops biting on the leash, immediately reward them with praise and a treat. This reinforces the desired behavior and strengthens the connection between not biting and the reward.

Continued training: Continue working on leash manners and general obedience training with your dog to improve their behavior in the long term. Set clear expectations and consistently reward them for good behavior.

Walks

Taking your Boxer for a walk holds significant importance for several reasons. Firstly, it grants your Boxer the opportunity to exercise, vital for their physical health and overall well-being. Regular walks aid in preventing obesity, fortifying muscles, and promoting joint mobility.

Moreover, walking is crucial for your Boxer's mental stimulation. Outdoors, they encounter diverse environments and partake in social interactions with fellow dogs and people, fostering mental enrichment and alleviating boredom and behavioral issues.

As a Boxer owner, walking also confers numerous benefits upon you. It strengthens the bond with your Boxer as you spend quality time together and deepen your connection. Additionally, it presents an opportunity for you to stay active and relish fresh air, positively impacting your own health and well-being.

Senses & Stimuli

During walks, your dog's senses are stimulated in various ways, leading to a profound experience and enriching their perception of the world.

Sense of Smell: Dogs heavily rely on their sense of smell, and walking provides a plethora of new scents to explore. From the scent of fresh flowers to the traces of other animals, there is a variety of olfactory stimuli that can fascinate your dog. For example, while walking through the park, your dog might track the trail of a squirrel or pick up the smell of a nearby barbecue.

Sense of Sight: There's much to see during a walk, whether it's the bustling activity on the street, other dogs passing by, or birds flying through the air. Your dog can visually explore its surroundings, directing attention to interesting movements or colors. Perhaps they'll spot a cat perched on a wall or watch with fascination as a ball flies through the air.

Sense of Touch: Walking on different surfaces like grass, asphalt, or sand also stimulates your dog's sense of touch. The feeling of grass under their paws or the cool earth can be pleasant and encourage them to further explore their surroundings.

Sense of Hearing: Walking is often surrounded by sounds, whether it's birds chirping, leaves rustling in the wind, or the hum of passing cars. All these sounds stimulate your dog's sense of hearing, offering a rich auditory experience. They might hear another dog barking and respond to it or notice the ringing of a bicycle bell and curiously stop.

How often should I walk my dog?

The frequency of walks depends on various factors, including the age, health condition, and energy levels of your dog. Generally, most dogs require at least two to three walks a day to get enough exercise and mental stimulation. It's important to consider the needs of your individual dog and adjust their walking schedule accordingly.

How long should a walk last?

The duration of the walk can vary depending on your dog's needs, but as a rule of thumb, most walks should last at least 30 minutes to an hour. High-energy dogs or those with a lot of excess energy may benefit from longer walks, while older dogs or puppies may require shorter walks. It's important to respect your dog's physical limits and not overexert them.

What can I do to keep my dog entertained during the walk?

There are many ways to keep your dog entertained and stimulated during the walk. For example, you could play interactive games like fetch or hide and seek to challenge their mind. Bringing along treats or toys can also help motivate and entertain your dog during the walk. Changing up the routes and exploring new environments can also help stimulate your dog mentally and provide them with new experiences.

How can I ensure my dog's safety during the walk?

Ensuring your dog's safety during the walk is of utmost importance. Keep them away from busy roads and dangerous areas, and watch out for potential hazards like toxic plants or aggressive animals. Using reflective materials or LED collars can also help improve your dog's visibility during nighttime walks.

Toys

In the world of dogs, few things bring as much happiness as toys. Whether it's a squeaky ball, a plush stuffed animal, or a sturdy chew toy, toys are an essential part of a dog's life. They provide not just entertainment, but also mental stimulation, exercise, and comfort.

The Importance of Toys

Playing with toys is of great importance for dogs as it has a variety of positive effects on their physical and mental health. First and foremost, toys allow dogs to unleash their natural energy and engage in physical activity. By running, jumping, and romping with their toys, dogs can strengthen their muscles, improve their endurance, and support their cardiovascular system. This not only contributes to physical fitness but can also help prevent obesity and related health issues.

Furthermore, playing with toys provides dogs with important mental stimulation. Interactive toys that require dogs to think, act strategically, and solve problems promote mental agility and keep the dog's mind active. This type of mental challenge is particularly important for avoiding boredom and promoting the dog's well-being.

Another benefit of playing with toys is promoting dental health. Many toys are specifically designed to support dogs' natural chewing behavior while also cleaning their teeth. Chewing on appropriate toys can help remove plaque and prevent gum disease, ultimately improving the dog's oral health.

Additionally, playing with toys can help alleviate anxiety and stress in dogs. Chewing on a favorite toy or interacting with a familiar object can have a calming effect and provide the dog with a sense of security, especially in stressful situations or when left alone.

In addition to the physical and mental benefits, playing with toys also fosters the bond between dog and owner. Shared playtimes create positive interactions and strengthen the trust and relationship between dog and human. These shared activities promote mutual understanding and connection, which in turn improves the dog's well-being and quality of life.

Safety First

Dog toys should be carefully inspected for potential hazards. This includes checking for loose parts, such as buttons or eyes, that could easily be torn off and swallowed. Sharp edges or seams should also be avoided to prevent injuries to the dog's mouth or paws. Additionally, toys intended for chewing should be made of non-toxic materials, as some plastics or dyes can be harmful if ingested by the dog.

The size of the toy is crucial for the dog's safety. Toys should be large enough to not be swallowed, but not so large that the dog struggles to handle or chew them. A toy that is too small poses a choking hazard, especially for puppies, while a toy that is too large can cause injuries if the dog carries it around or plays with it.

Although toys are designed for dogs, unexpected problems can still arise when the dog plays with them. A part of the toy could come loose or break off, posing a risk of choking or suffocation. For this reason, the dog owner should always be present during playtime with their dog to monitor the situation and intervene if necessary.

Types of Toys

Dogs, with their boundless energy and playful nature, adore toys. Each type of toy serves a unique purpose, offering both fun and benefits to your dog.

Chew Toys: Chew toys are perfect for dogs who love to gnaw and chew. These toys come in various shapes, sizes, and materials, from rubber bones to nylon chew toys. Chewing is not just enjoyable for dogs; it also helps to keep their teeth clean and healthy by removing plaque and tartar buildup. Plus, chewing can be a soothing activity for dogs, especially puppies who are teething.

Squeaky Toys: Squeaky toys are a favorite among many dogs. The irresistible sound of a squeaker can keep them entertained for hours on end. These toys often come in the form of plush animals or balls, and dogs love the challenge of making the squeak sound again and again. Squeaky toys stimulate a dog's natural hunting instincts and provide mental stimulation as they try to "catch" the sound.

Interactive Toys: Interactive toys are designed to engage a dog's mind and keep them entertained for extended periods. These toys often involve a puzzle or challenge that the dog must solve to access a treat or toy hidden inside. For example, a puzzle feeder toy might require a dog to manipulate levers or spinners to release kibble. These toys are excellent for keeping dogs mentally sharp and preventing boredom.

Fetch Toys: Fetch toys are perfect for dogs who love to run and play fetch with their humans. These toys typically include balls, frisbees, or sticks that can be thrown for a dog to retrieve. Fetch toys provide both physical exercise and mental stimulation as dogs chase after the toy and bring it back to their owner. They're a great way to burn off excess energy.

Tug Toys: Tug toys are perfect for interactive play between dogs and their owners. These toys often come in the form of ropes or rubber rings that dogs can grip with their teeth while their owners tug on the other end. Tug-of-war games are not only fun for dogs but also help to strengthen their jaw muscles.

Soft Toys: Soft toys, such as plush animals or blankets, provide comfort and security for dogs, especially puppies. Many dogs enjoy cuddling up with a soft toy for naptime or carrying it around as a security blanket. Soft toys can also be a source of entertainment, as dogs may shake, toss, or chew on them during playtime.

It's also important to rotate your dog's toys regularly to keep them interested and prevent boredom. Introducing new toys periodically adds variety to their playtime and keeps them engaged.

The Bonding Power of Toys

Toys aren't just for dogs; they're also a way for humans to bond with their furry companions. Playing with your dog strengthens your relationship and builds trust and affection between you. Whether it's tossing a ball in the backyard or playing a game of tug-of-war, spending quality time together with toys creates lasting memories and reinforces the special bond you share.

Advanced commands

Advanced commands play a pivotal role in a Boxer's development for several reasons. They not only provide mental stimulation but also foster cognitive health by engaging their minds and preventing boredom or behavioral issues stemming from under-stimulation. Moreover, advanced commands strengthen the bond between Boxers and their owners, showcasing a heightened level of trust and cooperation, thereby deepening communication and fortifying the relationship.

From a standpoint of safety and control, advanced commands empower owners to interact safely and efficiently with their Boxer in diverse situations. Commands like "Leave it" can deter the Boxer from approaching hazardous objects, while "No" communicates to the Boxer that their behavior is unacceptable at that moment. This affords owners greater control and safety over their Boxer's conduct.

Advanced commands also streamline daily life by facilitating smoother interactions between the Boxer and their owner, enabling them to accomplish tasks more effectively. Through commands such as "Shake," "High Five," or "Roll Over," the Boxer can execute various tricks, enhancing their training and mental stimulation. Additionally, a command like "Heel" teaches the Boxer to walk beside their owner and follow them during walks.

Ultimately, advanced commands equip the Boxer with a more adaptable and flexible response to diverse situations. A Boxer proficient in advanced commands is better prepared to navigate new environments, interact with different people, and address varying demands. This proves invaluable in a world characterized by constant change and diverse challenges.

Heel

The "heel" command is an essential part of dog training aimed at teaching the dog to walk alongside its owner without pulling on the leash or forging ahead. This command is crucial in numerous everyday situations. When walking through busy streets, the "heel" command can help keep the dog calm and controlled, preventing it from darting around wildly, which could startle passersby. Similarly, it is useful when taking a dog to a park where other dogs are running around. Through the "heel" command, the dog learns to behave calmly and not rush excitedly toward other dogs, thus avoiding conflicts.

Another example is visiting a café or restaurant with the dog. If the dog masters the "heel" command, it can lie quietly under the table and not try to approach other guests or snatch food. This allows for a pleasant and stress-free experience for the owner and other patrons.

Overall, learning the "heel" command helps the dog stay attentive to its owner. Additionally, it promotes safety, as a dog that stays by its owner's side is less susceptible to accidents or conflicts with other dogs.

Step by Step Introduction:

- Start with your dog in a sitting position beside you. Hold the leash in your preferred hand, keeping it short enough to maintain control but with enough slack to allow your dog to move comfortably.
- With your dog in the sitting position, give the command "heel" in a clear and firm tone. Use a hand signal, such as patting your leg or holding your hand close to your body, to further reinforce the command visually.

- Begin walking forward slowly, encouraging your dog to follow beside you. Use the leash to guide your dog's movement, keeping them close to your side. As you walk, maintain a steady pace and avoid sudden movements that may startle or confuse your dog.
- As your dog walks calmly beside you, praise them enthusiastically and offer occasional treats as rewards. Positive reinforcement helps your dog associate the behavior of walking calmly beside you with a positive outcome.
- If your dog starts to pull ahead or lag behind, gently guide them back into the correct position using the leash and reinforce the "heel" command.

Remember that teaching your dog to heel requires patience and persistence. Every dog learns at their own pace, so be patient with your dog's progress and celebrate their achievements along the way.

Leave It or No

The command "leave it" or "lass es" is an essential part of dog training as it teaches them to ignore potentially dangerous or unwanted objects and behaviors. This command has the potential to be lifesaving by encouraging dogs to avoid things that could be harmful to their health or safety.

An example of this is when a dog finds something on the street that seems enticing to it, such as a piece of chocolate or medication. In such cases, the "leave it" command can prevent the dog from ingesting these potentially toxic substances by signaling it to stay away from them.

Furthermore, the "leave it" command can also help stop unwanted behavior. For example, if a dog tends to rummage through the trash or search for leftovers, consistent training with the "leave it" command can teach it to refrain from this behavior and instead exhibit appropriate behavior.

The "leave it" command is also useful for protecting dogs from physical dangers. If a dog tries to investigate dangerous objects such as sharp edges or falling tablecloths, the "leave it" command can help prevent injuries by keeping the dog from exposing itself to these hazards.

During walks, the "leave it" command can be used to prevent dogs from following other stimuli such as passing animals or interesting smells. This helps keep the dog focused and under control, leading to a more pleasant and safer walking experience overall.

Difference between Drop it and Leave it /No

A fundamental difference between the commands "Drop it" and "Leave it" lies in their respective application and associated goals in dog training. "Drop it" is used to prompt the dog to release or let go of an object already in its mouth, particularly when the dog is holding something potentially dangerous or harmful. The aim of "Drop it" is to teach the dog to release items upon the handler's command, thus preventing injuries or damages.

In contrast, "Leave it" is employed to prevent the dog from looking at, touching, or taking a specific object. This command is typically applied before the dog reaches or picks up the undesirable item. The primary goal of "Leave it" is to teach the dog to ignore certain stimuli or objects and instead focus on what the handler communicates or allows.

Step by Step Introduction:

- Start by holding a treat in your closed hand and presenting it to your dog. As your dog shows interest in the treat, firmly say the command "leave it" or "no" in a clear and assertive tone.
- As soon as you issue the command, quickly redirect your dog's attention away from the treat by offering them a different treat from your other hand. This teaches your dog that ignoring the forbidden item results in a positive reward.
- When your dog refrains from trying to obtain the forbidden item and focuses on the treat in your other hand, immediately praise them and give them the alternative treat as a reward. Positive reinforcement helps your dog understand the desired behavior.
- Repeat the "leave it" or "no" command and redirection process several times during each training session. Start

with easy-to-ignore items and gradually increase the difficulty by using more tempting objects.

- As your dog becomes more proficient, increase the distance between them and the forbidden item. Practice the command from a few inches away, gradually working up to greater distances. Additionally, extend the duration of the "leave it" or "no" command, requiring your dog to maintain their focus for longer periods before receiving the reward.
- Once your dog has mastered the command in controlled settings, incorporate real-life scenarios into your training. For example, practice "leave it" or "no" when encountering food scraps on walks or when your dog tries to grab something off the counter at home.

Differences between Leave it & No

"Leave it" is typically applied before the dog reaches or picks up the undesirable object. It teaches the dog to ignore certain stimuli or objects on command from the owner, focusing instead on what is permitted or what the owner communicates. In contrast, "No" is a general interruptive command signaling to the dog that its behavior is not acceptable in that moment. It can be used for a variety of undesirable behaviors, not just responding to specific objects or stimuli.

When Not to Use Leave It

The "Leave it" command should be used judiciously, as there are situations where its application may not be appropriate:

Natural Behaviors: In some cases, ignoring certain stimuli or objects that are part of the dog's natural behaviors may be inappropriate or even harmful. For example, "Leave it" should not be used to prevent the dog from scratching, sniffing, or performing other normal behaviors unless medically necessary.

Training Situations: If the dog is in a training situation where it's important for him to explore or interact with different stimuli or objects, using "Leave it" could hinder the learning process or affect the dog's trust in his environment and owner.

It's important to use the "Leave it" command judiciously and in the context of each situation to ensure that it helps the dog behave appropriately while respecting his natural needs and behaviors.

Shake

The command "Shake" is a valuable skill commonly taught during dog obedience training. It involves the dog offering its paw on command and placing it in the hand of the human. This simple yet effective skill carries a variety of benefits that are advantageous for both the dog and the owner.

Furthermore, the "Shake" command provides another avenue to promote the dog's obedience. Learning new commands and tricks helps stimulate the dog's mental faculties and improve its behavior. When the dog learns to offer its paw on command, it demonstrates not only obedience but also the ability to learn new things and follow instructions.

The dog's coordination and fine motor skills are also enhanced through training the "Shake" command. By learning to lift its paw purposefully and place it in the owner's hand, the dog develops better control over its movements. This increased dexterity can prove useful in other areas of the dog's life as well.

For a dog owner, there may be situations where the "Shake" command is particularly helpful. For example, it can be practical for the dog to learn to wipe its paws before entering the house to reduce dirt and moisture. Additionally, the "Shake" command can also be useful in situations such as visiting the veterinarian or trimming nails by helping the dog remain calm and have a positive interaction with the owner

Step by Step Introduction:

- With the treat in your hand, extend your palm towards your dog, keeping it low enough for them to reach comfortably. This gesture encourages your dog to paw at your hand in an attempt to reach the treat.
- As your dog makes a pawing motion towards your hand, say the command "shake" in a clear and firm voice. Timing is crucial here – it's essential to utter the command at the exact moment your dog extends their paw towards you.
- The moment your dog's paw makes contact with your hand, praise them enthusiastically and give them the treat as a reward. Positive reinforcement helps your dog associate the action of shaking paws with a positive outcome.

- Repeat the "shake" command several times during each training session, rewarding your dog for each successful attempt. Keep the sessions short and engaging to maintain your dog's interest and motivation.
- Once your dog consistently offers their paw in response to the hand gesture, add a verbal cue to the command. Say "shake" just before presenting your hand, gradually phasing out the hand gesture until your dog responds to the verbal cue alone.
- Once your dog has mastered shaking with one paw, encourage them to shake with the other paw as well. Use the same steps as before, offering praise and rewards for each successful attempt.

When Not to Use 'Shake' Command

Aggressive Behavior: If a dog is already showing signs of aggression, such as growling, baring teeth, or rapid body movements, it is not advisable to use the "Shake" command. Lifting the paw could be interpreted as a threat and lead to aggressive behavior.

Physical Limitations: If a dog has injuries or suffers from a physical limitation such as arthritis, lifting the paw could cause pain or worsen the condition. In such cases, it is better not to strain the dog and refrain from training the "Shake" command until the veterinarian gives the green light.

Fear or Uncertainty: If a dog is fearful or uncertain, lifting the paw may further unsettle it or trigger flight reactions. In such cases, it is important to build the dog's confidence before attempting to train the "Shake" command.

Unwanted Behavior: If the dog misunderstands the "Shake" command and associates it with unwanted behavior such as scratching or jumping, the training should be reconsidered and adjusted. It is important to clearly communicate which actions are rewarded and which are not.

Roll Over

The roll-over command is not just a simple trick for dogs, but a versatile training technique with a variety of benefits for both the dog and the owner. Learning the roll-over command not only develops physical abilities but also provides mental stimulation and fosters a deeper bond between the dog and the owner.

Firstly, the roll-over command promotes the dog's physical activity and mobility. By teaching the dog to turn and roll onto its back on command, various muscle groups are engaged, and flexibility is improved. This can be particularly useful for maintaining the mobility of older dogs or helping young dogs strengthen their muscles and joints.

In addition to these fundamental benefits, the roll-over command can be helpful in a variety of everyday situations. For example, it can help calm and relax the dog, which can be particularly useful when the dog is stressed or anxious.

Furthermore, the roll-over command can also be useful in situations such as vet visits or grooming. By teaching the dog to lie down and roll over on command, examinations and treatments can be performed more easily, reducing stress for both the dog and the owner.

Step by Step Introduction:
- Ask your dog to lie down on their side. If your dog is not familiar with the "down" command, you may need to practice this first. Use treats and praise to encourage your dog to lie down on their side.
- Once your dog is in the lying down position, hold a treat in your hand and position it near their nose. Slowly move the

treat in a circular motion towards their shoulder, encouraging them to follow the movement with their head.

- As your dog follows the treat with their nose, continue moving the treat in a circular motion towards their back, encouraging them to roll onto their back. Use a verbal cue such as "roll over" to associate the action with the command.

- The moment your dog completes the roll-over motion and ends up lying on their back, praise them enthusiastically and give them the treat as a reward. Positive reinforcement helps your dog associate the action of rolling over with a positive outcome.

- Repeat the roll-over command several times during each training session, rewarding your dog for each successful attempt. Keep the sessions short and engaging to maintain your dog's interest and motivation.

- Once your dog consistently rolls over in response to the hand gesture, add a verbal cue to the command. Say "roll over" just before presenting the treat, gradually phasing out the hand gesture until your dog responds to the verbal cue alone.

- Encourage your dog to roll over from both sides by alternating the direction of the roll. Use the same steps as before, offering praise and rewards for each successful attempt.

Specialized Training

So, after successfully mastering the advanced commands, we can now turn our attention to the specialized areas of dog training. In this section, we will delve deeper into crate training, clicker training, and mental stimulation before moving on to various dog sports.

Crate Training

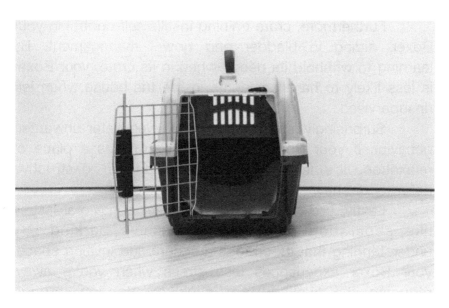

Crate training holds immense importance for Boxers for a multitude of reasons. One crucial aspect is safety. Familiarizing your Boxer with staying in its crate when unsupervised reduces the risk of injury to itself or your belongings, particularly vital if you have a curious puppy eager to explore everything.

Teaching your Boxer to feel secure and at ease in its crate provides a haven for relaxation and stress relief, particularly beneficial during thunderstorms, fireworks, or when guests are over. Offering your Boxer its own sanctuary to retreat to promotes a sense of security and aids in calming anxious nerves.

Additionally, crate training aids in acclimating your Boxer to novel situations. When already accustomed to its secure space, your Boxer will find it easier to feel comfortable while traveling or during vet visits.

Crate training transcends mere retreat provision; it plays a pivotal role in nurturing emotional stability and adaptability in varied circumstances.

Furthermore, crate training instills self-control in your Boxer, aiding in bladder and bowel management. By learning to withhold its needs when in its crate, your Boxer is less likely to have accidents inside the house when left unsupervised.

Surprisingly, crate training can even deter unwanted behavior. If your Boxer perceives its crate as a place of relaxation, it's less inclined to engage in destructive behavior or chew on items in your absence.

Lastly, crate training can mitigate behavioral issues like separation anxiety or excessive barking. By understanding that its crate is a secure and inviting space, your Boxer experiences less stress when you're away, reducing the likelihood of seeking attention through incessant barking.

Choose the right Crate

Choosing the right crate for your dog's crate training is a crucial step, especially if you're a new dog owner and not sure what to look for. Here are some key aspects to consider when selecting the perfect crate for your dog:

Size: The size of the crate is crucial. It should be large enough for your dog to comfortably stand, lie down, and turn around. A general rule is that the crate should be about the length of your dog plus half of its height. This gives your dog enough space to move around but not so much that it uses the crate as a toilet.

Material: Crates come in various materials such as wire, plastic, and fabric. Wire crates provide good ventilation and allow good visibility for your dog, which can help prevent it from feeling too isolated. Plastic crates are often cozier and more secure as they have less air circulation, but they may also offer less light and visibility. Fabric crates are lightweight and portable, but they may be less sturdy and offer less security.

Safety: Make sure the crate is safe and has no sharp edges or protruding parts that could injure your dog. Pay particular attention to ensuring that the door closes securely and does not accidentally open to prevent your dog from escaping or getting injured.

Portability: If you plan to take the crate with you often, choose one that is lightweight and easy to fold or disassemble. This makes it easier to transport and store the crate when not in use.

Adaptability: Some dogs feel safer in a covered crate, while others prefer a more open one. Some crates come with covers or blankets that you can use to customize the crate to your dog's preferences. Experiment with different options to find out what works best for your dog.

One for home and one for the car?

It's entirely possible and often practical to purchase the same crate twice and use one at home while the other stays in the car. This option offers several advantages and makes organization easier for you and the comfort of your dog. By owning two identical crates, one for home and one for the car, you create a consistent environment for your dog no matter where it is. This can help minimize its stress and provide it with a sense of familiarity and security, both during the journey and at the destination.

Using the same crate in both environments also allows your dog to recognize its own scent and adapt quickly to its new surroundings. This can be especially helpful when traveling with your dog or taking it to different places. From a practical standpoint, owning two identical crates also facilitates organization. You don't have to move the crate back and forth between the house and the car each time but have a permanent solution for both locations.

If you decide to purchase the same crate twice, make sure it fits well both at home and in the car and meets your dog's needs. Ensure that both crates are securely fastened to prevent accidents and clean them regularly to remove dirt and odors.

Step by Step Introduction:

- Introducing your dog to a new transport crate is an important step in providing it with a safe and comfortable feeling in its new environment. It's crucial to proceed with patience and empathy to ensure that your dog perceives the crate as a positive place.
- First and foremost, it's important to present the transport crate as a place of safety and comfort. Place the crate in a quiet area of the house, away from high-traffic areas, to provide your dog with a calm environment to explore. Place some of its favorite toys or a soft cushion inside to make the crate inviting.
- Use treats or food to encourage your dog to voluntarily enter the crate. Leave the door open so it feels secure and can explore the crate at its own pace. Praise and reward it abundantly each time it enters the crate to create positive associations.
- Once your dog feels comfortable, you can slowly begin to close the door for short periods while it's inside the crate. Then, immediately open it again and reward it with treats and praise. This step should be gradual, with the duration of time the door remains closed gradually increasing. It's important for your dog to learn that closing the door is not a threat and that it's safe even when temporarily confined in the crate.

- Throughout this process, it's essential to have patience and respect your dog's needs. Every dog is unique and will react differently to being introduced to the transport crate. Some dogs will quickly acclimate to the crate, while others may need more time. Take the time your dog needs and encourage it with positive reinforcement and patience.
- Avoid using the crate as a form of punishment, as this could evoke negative feelings and affect the introduction process. Instead, present the crate as a place of peace and comfort where your dog can voluntarily retreat.

Nighttime Crating

Sleeping in a crate at night can offer many benefits for your dog. Firstly, the crate provides your dog with its own safe space, giving it a sense of security. This is particularly important as dogs are naturally den animals and feel secure in tight, protected areas. A crate can fulfill this need for a sheltered sleeping area.

Moreover, using a crate can reduce the risk of nighttime accidents, as many dogs tend to keep their own sleeping environment clean. By having your dog sleep in a crate, you also provide it with clear structure and routine, which can be conducive to its sleep cycle.

Initially placing the crate in your bedroom can help your dog adjust more quickly to its new sleeping arrangement. The proximity to you during the night can provide it with additional security. After a while, once your dog feels comfortable, you can gradually move the crate to the desired location.

Troubleshooting

If your dog exhibits signs of distress or anxiety when in the crate, such as excessive whining or barking, take a step back and proceed more slowly. Revisit earlier steps in the training process and gradually reintroduce your dog to the crate using positive reinforcement techniques. Additionally, ensure your dog's physical and mental needs are adequately met, including sufficient exercise and mental stimulation.

Clicker Training

Clicker training proves highly effective for Boxers, aiding in shaping their behavior and fostering obedience. This method revolves around a distinct clicking sound, signaling to the Boxer that it has executed a desired action and merits a reward. Widely embraced by professional trainers and dog owners worldwide, clicker training proves invaluable in various realms, including obedience, tricks, behavior correction, and addressing fears or insecurities.

The efficacy of clicker training stems from its ability to offer precise feedback and leverage positive reinforcement. By consistently producing a distinct sound, the clicker swiftly teaches the Boxer which behaviors yield rewards. This facilitates swift and efficient learning as the Boxer forms associations between its actions and the ensuing rewards.

In everyday scenarios, clicker training proves instrumental in teaching basic obedience. When instructing the Boxer to respond to cues like "sit" or "down," the clicker marks the precise moment when the Boxer assumes the desired posture. Coupled with rewards such as treats or praise, the Boxer swiftly grasps that compliance leads to rewards, motivating it to replicate the behavior.

Similarly, clicker training can address undesirable behaviors. For instance, if your Boxer tends to pull on the leash, the clicker can signify the instant it ceases pulling and walks calmly by your side. By pairing the clicker with positive reinforcement, you effectively convey to your Boxer that leash manners are rewarded, encouraging the display of desirable behavior over time.

Step by Step Introduction:

A clicker is a simple tool that produces a distinct clicking sound when you press it. This sound will serve as a signal to your dog, indicating that it has performed the desired behavior correctly. You can purchase a clicker at most pet stores or online.

Once you have your clicker, it's time to familiarize your dog with it. Sit with your dog in a quiet place where you won't be disturbed. Press the clicker and simultaneously give your dog a treat. Repeat this process several times so that your dog associates the clicking sound with something positive, like a treat.

After your dog understands the clicker, it's time to start the actual training. Choose a simple behavior you want to teach your dog, such as sitting. Wait patiently until your dog naturally exhibits the desired behavior. Once it does, press the clicker and immediately give it a treat as a reward.

It's important that you click and reward at the right time, namely, precisely when your dog displays the desired behavior. This helps your dog quickly learn that the clicking sound is a positive signal followed by a reward.

Repeat this process several times until your dog reliably exhibits the behavior in response to the clicker. Then, you can add a cue to give the command, such as "sit." Say the cue just before your dog performs the behavior, then click and reward it.

Use various rewards and gradually increase the difficulty by, for example, increasing distractions or practicing the behavior in different environments.

Mental Stimulation

Mental stimulation holds immense significance for Boxers, offering a plethora of benefits that extend beyond physical well-being. Insufficient mental stimulation can lead to boredom, restlessness, and even feelings of depression in Boxers, highlighting the importance of this form of enrichment.

Boxers, by nature, are inherently curious and intelligent creatures. They possess an innate drive to explore their surroundings and acquire new knowledge. Nurturing this intelligence through regular mental stimulation is vital for fostering healthy cognitive development in Boxers.

Moreover, mental stimulation serves a pivotal role in averting behavioral problems. Boxers deprived of adequate mental enrichment may resort to undesirable behaviors such as destructive chewing, incessant barking, aggression, or other behavioral issues. By engaging their minds through various forms of mental stimulation, Boxers can channel their energy constructively and exhibit more balanced behavior.

Benefits of Puzzles and Games:

Puzzles and games are essential components to promote the mental stimulation of dogs. By engaging in puzzles, finding hidden treats, and mastering challenges, dogs enhance their cognitive abilities. These activities require concentration, problem-solving skills, and strategic thinking, which in turn increase their mental agility.

Types of Puzzles and Games

Intelligence Toys: There are various types of intelligence toys that require different levels of thinking skills.

Some involve simple tasks like lifting flaps or turning wheels, while others require more complex problem-solving, such as moving obstacles to access rewards. By gradually increasing the difficulty, you can continuously challenge and improve your dog's cognitive performance.

Snuffle Mats: These mats can be divided into different difficulty levels based on how tightly the fibers are woven and how well the treats are hidden. You can also use various materials to stimulate your dog's senses. Some snuffle mats even have hidden pockets or compartments that need to be opened to access the reward, increasing the challenge.

Hide and Seek: In addition to simply hiding treats, you can also incorporate hiding objects or even yourself as a game. This not only stimulates the dog's sense of smell but also its ability to find and recognize complex hiding spots.

Obedience Games: In addition to basic obedience exercises, you can practice more advanced tasks such as finding specific objects by name or performing commands in specific sequences. These activities not only promote cognitive stimulation but also strengthen the bond between dog and owner.

Interactive Toys: Some interactive toys require the dog to perform certain movements to access the reward, such as pushing or turning parts. You can also use toys that produce sounds or lights to grab the dog's attention and stimulate its senses.

Thinking Games: These games can be divided into various categories, such as puzzle boards where the dog has to pull out pegs or interactive toys that require pulling out drawers.

Learning Games: Practicing new skills, such as opening doors or pulling ropes, not only requires cognitive effort but also promotes your dog's fine motor skills and coordination.

Dog sports

Engaging in sports is vital for Boxers to uphold both their physical fitness and mental well-being. Much like humans, regular physical activity is key to staving off obesity, boosting endurance, and mitigating the risk of health ailments like heart disease, diabetes, and joint issues. Sports empower Boxers to fortify their muscles and joints, crucial for averting mobility challenges as they mature.

Beyond the evident physical perks, sports yield myriad psychological advantages for Boxers. Physical exertion enables them to dispel energy and alleviate stress, fostering positive behavior and mental equilibrium. Moreover, the mental stimulation inherent in training enhances cognitive agility and combats boredom, curbing undesirable behaviors like excessive barking or destructiveness.

Sporting pursuits also furnish avenues for social interaction for Boxers, be it frolicking with fellow canines or participating in activities alongside their owners. From leisurely strolls to demanding endeavors such as agility or swimming, Boxers have an array of options tailored to their abilities and inclinations. By incorporating diverse activities and integrating training into their routine, owners ensure their Boxers remain fit, hearty, and jubilant.

It's imperative to acknowledge that like humans, Boxers necessitate an appropriate level of physical exertion, as excessive activity can yield adverse effects. Overexertion may predispose certain breeds, especially puppies or those with genetic propensities to joint ailments like hip or elbow dysplasia, to joint problems. Furthermore, excessive exercise can incite a literal addiction to movement, compelling Boxers to persist in activity despite exhaustion or discomfort.

As responsible custodians, it behooves owners to monitor their Boxer's activity levels attentively and ensure they align with their pet's needs and thresholds. This entails heeding cues of fatigue and providing ample rest and recuperation intervals. Regular veterinary check-ups are paramount to ascertain the Boxer's well-being and stave off signs of overexertion or injury.

A harmonious blend of physical activity, mental stimulation, and rest intervals is pivotal for a Boxer's holistic well-being. By catering to their pet's requisites and striking a balanced equilibrium between activity and repose, owners safeguard that their Boxers remain vigorous, hale, and exuberant, without overstraining or underwhelming them.

Jogging

Jogging can be an extremely beneficial form of physical activity for dogs, with numerous positive effects on their health and well-being. This is especially important for dogs prone to obesity or with lower activity levels, as jogging can help shed excess pounds and improve overall physical condition.

Furthermore, jogging provides valuable mental stimulation for dogs. While running, dogs can explore new environments, perceive different scents, and engage their senses, contributing to their mental well-being. Interaction with the natural environment can be highly enriching for dogs, helping them to mentally exhaust themselves.

Shared activities like jogging can strengthen trust and the bond between the dog and their owner. This not only enhances the relationship but can also help reduce behavioral problems often stemming from excess energy.

However, it's important to note that not all dogs are equally suited for jogging. Factors such as physical condition, age and any existing health issues should be considered before starting training. A slow and gradual introduction to jogging is crucial to avoid injuries and ensure the dog can handle the strain appropriately. Additionally, it's essential to monitor the dog's needs during the run and ensure they don't overexert or overheat.

Step by Step Introduction:

- Start by introducing your dog to the concept of jogging in a controlled environment such as your backyard or a quiet park. Begin with short, slow-paced sessions to gauge your dog's interest and comfort level. Use positive reinforcement techniques such as treats, praise, and encouragement to make jogging a positive experience for your dog.
- Teach your dog to walk or run calmly beside you using a loose leash. Practice leash manners and basic obedience commands such as "heel" and "stay" to ensure your dog remains under control during jogging sessions. Gradually increase the pace and duration of your runs as your dog becomes more accustomed to jogging on leash.
- Prior to each jogging session, warm up your dog's muscles with a brisk walk or gentle stretching exercises. After the run, allow your dog to cool down gradually by walking and stretching to prevent muscle soreness and injuries.
- Pay attention to your dog's form and technique while jogging to ensure they maintain a comfortable and efficient stride. Avoid excessive pulling or dragging on the leash, and monitor your dog's breathing and energy levels throughout the run. Adjust your pace and distance

accordingly to accommodate your dog's fitness level and endurance.

- Provide ample opportunities for your dog to drink water before, during, and after jogging to prevent dehydration. Additionally, ensure your dog's diet is well-balanced and provides the necessary nutrients to support their energy needs as an active runner.
- Gradually increase the intensity and duration of your jogging sessions over time to build your dog's endurance and stamina. Pay attention to any signs of fatigue or discomfort and adjust your training plan accordingly to prevent overexertion and injuries.
- Above all, prioritize your dog's enjoyment and well-being while jogging together. Pay attention to their body language and cues to ensure they're having a positive experience. Use jogging as an opportunity to strengthen your bond with your dog and enjoy the great outdoors together.

How can I teach my dog to jog alongside me without pulling on the leash?

Start with short walks or slow jogging sessions, and reward your dog for staying close to you. Use a harness to minimize pressure on the neck and a leash that gives you enough control. Employ clear signals when your dog pulls and reward them for staying beside you. Repeat this training regularly and gradually increase the distance and speed.

Should I take certain precautions when jogging with my dog in hot weather?

Jogging in hot weather can be dangerous for dogs as they can easily overheat. It's important to minimize the strain on your dog and take certain precautions. Plan your jogging sessions during the cooler hours of the day, such as early morning or late evening. Avoid hot surfaces like asphalt, as they can burn your dog's paws. Bring enough water for your dog and take regular breaks to allow them to cool down. Watch out for signs of overheating such as excessive panting, lethargy, or vomiting, and seek veterinary help immediately if needed.

Is jogging still a suitable activity for my older dog?

When it comes to older dogs, it's important to consider their individual needs and abilities. While some older dogs may still be able to handle slow and short jogging sessions, it's advisable to consult with a veterinarian beforehand to ensure your dog is healthy enough for this activity. Older dogs may be more prone to joint issues, arthritis, or other health problems that could affect jogging. It's important to take their physical condition into account and consider alternative activities that are less strenuous, such as moderate-paced walks or swimming.

What signs indicate that my dog is overexerted while jogging?

An overexerted dog may exhibit various signs indicating that they need a break or that jogging is too intense for them. These signs include heavy panting, excessive drooling, tongue hanging out, limping, weakness, disinterest in running, hobbling, sudden slowing of pace, unusual behavior such as constant stopping or lying down while running. If you notice such signs, it's important to immediately give your dog a break, offer them water, and observe them. If the symptoms persist or worsen, you should stop jogging and seek veterinary advice.

Are there certain diseases or health conditions where jogging may not be suitable for my dog?

Yes, there are certain health conditions or diseases where jogging may not be suitable for dogs. These include joint problems such as arthritis or hip dysplasia, heart conditions, respiratory diseases, obesity, injuries, or surgical interventions requiring restricted movement.

Flyball

The Flyball game is not just a simple pastime for dogs; it offers a variety of benefits that promote both physical and mental health. This fascinating dog sport is an exciting race that requires speed, agility, and teamwork.

First and foremost, Flyball is a fantastic way to improve your dog's physical fitness. The activity involves quick sprints, jumping over obstacles, and retrieving a ball. These movements not only contribute to increasing endurance but also strengthen muscles and improve the dog's agility. Just think about how often your dog sprints around in daily life, whether it's in the park, playing with other dogs, or even romping around in the garden. Flyball training can help channel this natural energy into a structured and positive activity.

Furthermore, Flyball provides valuable mental stimulation for your dog. Overcoming obstacles requires skill and concentration, while retrieving the ball is a targeted action. This cognitive challenge helps avoid boredom and promotes your dog's mental agility. For example, observing your dog finding new ways to reach its toys or solving small puzzles in everyday life showcases its natural curiosity and intelligence. Flyball training offers a structured way to further develop these skills while having fun.

Step by Step Introduction:

- Start by introducing your dog to the key equipment used in flyball, including hurdles and the flyball box. Begin with low hurdles and allow your dog to become familiar with jumping over them. Use positive reinforcement techniques such as treats, praise, and toys to encourage your dog's interaction with the equipment.

104

- Train your dog to retrieve a tennis ball reliably and return it to you on command. Use positive reinforcement to encourage your dog to bring the ball back to you consistently. Practice retrieving exercises both on and off the flyball course to reinforce good retrieval skills.
- Teach your dog to trigger the flyball box and catch the ball as it is ejected. Start by introducing your dog to the box at a distance and gradually decrease the distance as they become more comfortable. Use a combination of verbal cues and hand signals to guide your dog through the box turn sequence.
- Once your dog has mastered the individual components of flyball, introduce them to the concept of relay racing. Start by practicing short relay races with a single hurdle and the flyball box. Gradually increase the number of hurdles and the complexity of the course as your dog gains confidence and skill.
- Flyball is a team sport that requires precise timing and coordination between dogs and handlers. Practice timing your releases and recalls to ensure smooth transitions between dogs in the relay. Focus on building trust and communication with your dog to optimize your team's performance on the flyball course.
- Prepare for flyball competitions by simulating race conditions during training sessions. Practice racing against other teams and familiarize your dog with the sights and sounds of the competition environment. Focus on maintaining a positive and supportive atmosphere for your dog to thrive in the high-energy atmosphere of flyball competitions.
- Above all, prioritize your dog's enjoyment and well-being throughout the flyball training process. Celebrate their successes and milestones along the way, and always approach training with a spirit of sportsmanship and camaraderie. Whether you're competing or simply having

fun with your dog, flyball is an exhilarating sport that strengthens the bond between you and your canine companion.

What are the most common mistakes that dog owners make during Flyball training, and how can I avoid them?
One of the most common mistakes in Flyball training is overloading the dog with too fast or intense training. It's important to gradually increase training and give your dog enough breaks to recover. Another mistake is neglecting safety, such as using unsafe obstacles or not adequately considering the dog's physical health. Ensure that the training area is safe and free from injury hazards. Another common mistake is using negative reinforcement, like shouting or punishment, to control or motivate the dog. This can lead to fear or stress and affect the trust between you and your dog. Instead, use positive reinforcement techniques like rewards and praise to promote good behavior and maintain motivation.

How can I ensure that my dog safely overcomes the obstacles in Flyball?
Your dog's safety during Flyball play is paramount. To ensure that your dog safely overcomes obstacles, structured and well-monitored training is essential. Start with low obstacles and allow your dog to jump over them slowly and gently. Ensure that the obstacles are securely set up and have no sharp edges or loose parts that could cause injury.

What health considerations should I take into account before playing Flyball with my dog?
Before playing Flyball with your dog, it's important to ensure that they are physically fit and healthy. Flyball is an intense

physical activity that requires physical fitness and endurance. Check your dog for signs of injuries or illnesses that could affect their ability to play. Ensure that during training, your dog gets enough hydration and rest to avoid overexertion. Pause training immediately if your dog shows signs of exhaustion or discomfort.

How can I tell if my dog is having fun with Flyball or if they are overwhelmed?

Your dog's joy and motivation are crucial indicators of whether they are having fun with Flyball or not. Pay attention to their body language and behavior during training. A dog having fun with Flyball will be excited and engaged, with ears perked up, a wagging tail, and a smile on their face. They will actively participate in the game, enthusiastically retrieve the ball, and willingly jump over obstacles. A stressed or overwhelmed dog, on the other hand, may show signs of hesitation, restlessness, or fear. They might withdraw, flatten their ears, tuck their tail, or show signs of discomfort like panting or excessive licking. If you notice your dog is stressed or unhappy, adjust or pause the training to avoid overwhelming them.

Are there alternative games or activities I can try with my dog if they show no interest in Flyball?

If your dog shows no interest in Flyball, there are many alternative games and activities you can enjoy together. For example, you can play frisbee, engage in obedience training, take outdoor walks, or simply relax together. Every dog has different preferences and abilities, so it's important to find activities that match their individual temperament and interests. Experiment with different games and activities to find what your dog enjoys most and enjoy the time together.

How can I integrate Flyball training into my daily routine if I have a busy schedule?

You can incorporate short training sessions into your daily walks or playtime to integrate the activity into your routine. Remember that even short training sessions can be effective as long as they are consistently carried out. By integrating training into your daily routine, you can ensure that your dog receives regular exercise and both of you benefit from the advantages of Flyball play.

Herding

Dog Herding, a fascinating sport that harnesses the ancient skills of dogs working with livestock and translates them into a modern competitive environment. This sport is based on the centuries-old tradition of herding dogs, which are used to control and guide herds of livestock such as sheep, cattle, or goats. Originally a necessary practice for livestock farming on farms and in rural communities, Dog Herding has evolved into a popular dog sport in recent decades.

In Dog Herding with a ball as a training method, dogs showcase their innate abilities by guiding a ball through a designated course or arena. The dog's task is to move the ball precisely, follow the handler's instructions, and efficiently control the ball. This often involves overcoming obstacles, adhering to specific routes, or even isolating individual balls from the group - all under the guidance of their handler.

The challenge in Dog Herding with a ball lies not only in mastering the physical aspects of driving and guiding the ball but also in the close collaboration between dog and handler. Communication between the two is crucial, as the handler directs the dog's actions through gestures, whistles, or verbal commands. This symbiosis of human and dog, based on trust, respect, and mutual understanding, is the essence of Dog Herding.

While the actual utility of herding dogs on farms may not be as prominent today as in past times, their use in dog sports has proven to be extremely popular. Dog Herding competitions with a ball provide dog owners with an opportunity to showcase and test their dogs' natural abilities.

The diversity of Dog Herding competitions with a ball ranges from informal events at the local level to large international tournaments. Participants come from various backgrounds - from amateur dog owners to experienced professionals.

Step by Step Introduction:

- Find a suitable location for training. A large enclosed area without distractions is ideal, such as a fenced yard or a quiet park.
- Choose a ball that is suitable for your dog. A ball with a diameter of about 20 to 25 cm, sturdy enough to withstand your dog's biting, is recommended.
- Prepare tasty rewards that your dog enjoys. These can be small treats or toys that provide extra motivation for your dog.
- Start with simple exercises to teach your dog to fetch the ball. Roll the ball slowly on the ground and encourage your dog to chase after it.
- Gradually add verbal commands, such as "Fetch the ball" or "Bring the ball here," while encouraging your dog to retrieve the ball and bring it back.
- Praise and reward your dog extensively when he successfully fetches and retrieves the ball. Positive reinforcement is crucial for reinforcing the desired behavior.
- Gradually increase the difficulty by throwing the ball further or placing different obstacles in the training area to provide your dog with a greater challenge.
- Once your dog has learned to move the ball, you can perform exercises to improve his precision. Place objects such as cones or markers in the training area and challenge your dog to maneuver the ball around them.

- Train your dog to perform directional changes with the ball. This can be achieved through verbal commands like "right" and "left" while rolling the ball in the corresponding direction.
- Incorporate obstacles like low hurdles or small ramps into the training to test your dog's ability to drive the ball across different surfaces and overcome obstacles.
- Challenge your dog to drive the ball at increasing speeds. This can be achieved by throwing the ball further or encouraging your dog to run faster to catch the ball.
- Add variations to the training to increase your dog's mental stimulation. For example, hide the ball behind objects or have it roll through tunnels to further develop your dog's skills.

Can I train Dog Herding with a ball at home, or do I need special facilities?

Dog Herding with a ball can be trained both at home and in specialized training facilities, depending on the available resources and preferences of the dog owner. At home, you can use a safe area such as a fenced-in garden or a large living room to practice with your dog and develop basic skills. Specialized training facilities often provide additional amenities such as obstacles, sheep, or professional guidance to support and enhance training. The choice of training location depends on individual needs and goals.

Are there special techniques or strategies I can apply to optimize Dog Herding training?

To optimize Dog Herding training with a ball, various techniques and strategies can be employed. These include the use of different training methods such as clicker training or target training, varying tasks and exercises to mentally and physically challenge the dog, and gradual progression in training to continuously challenge and motivate the dog. It's also important to keep the training varied and interesting to maintain the dog's motivation and foster its willingness to learn.

How do I deal with frustration when my dog struggles with Dog Herding training?
Frustration is a natural part of the training process, both for the dog and the handler. If your dog is having difficulty or the training is not going as expected, it's important to remain patient and not lose your temper. Try to view the situation from your dog's perspective and focus on the positive progress. Take time to consider what adjustments can be made to the training to help your dog succeed.

Swimming

Dogs are naturally curious and active animals, and swimming allows them to indulge their natural instincts while improving their physical fitness.

Swimming is an extremely joint-friendly sport for dogs, as the water relieves the joints while simultaneously exercising the muscles. This form of movement is particularly beneficial for dogs with joint problems or older animals, as it is hardly stressful. Furthermore, swimming provides an ideal way to reduce overweight and improve endurance.

One of the most obvious reasons for the importance of swimming for dogs is the promotion of physical fitness. Similar to humans, regular exercise, such as swimming, can increase the dog's endurance and strength. Swimming engages various muscle groups, including legs, back, and shoulders, leading to overall stronger and healthier musculature.

This is especially important for dogs prone to joint problems such as arthritis or overweight, as the water supports their weight, thus reducing the strain on their joints. Swimming not only promotes physical fitness but also is enjoyable for many dogs, further boosting motivation for regular exercise.

Moreover, swimming provides an excellent opportunity for rehabilitation after injuries or surgical procedures. The buoyancy in the water reduces pressure on the affected areas, allowing the dog to strengthen its muscles and gradually restore its mobility without the risk of further injuries. Veterinarians often recommend swimming as part of the rehabilitation process for dogs with orthopedic problems or after surgery.

In addition to the physical benefits, swimming also has positive effects on the mental health of dogs. Many dogs enjoy playing and swimming in the water, providing them with a means to relax and relieve stress. This is particularly important for dogs that are anxious or nervous, as swimming can have a calming effect while simultaneously boosting their confidence.

Step by Step Introduction:

- Begin by introducing your dog to the water gradually, using positive reinforcement techniques such as treats, toys, and praise to create a positive association. Start in shallow water where your dog can wade comfortably, allowing them to explore and acclimate to the sensation of being in the water.
- Teach your dog to stay buoyant and maintain a relaxed, floating position in the water. Support your dog's body as needed and encourage them to relax their muscles and legs, allowing them to float naturally on the surface of the

114

water. Use gentle praise and encouragement to reassure your dog and build confidence in the water.

- Introduce basic swimming techniques to your dog, such as paddling with their legs and moving their arms in a circular motion. Start in shallow water where your dog can touch the bottom and gradually increase the depth as they become more comfortable and proficient at swimming. Use a flotation device or life jacket if needed to provide additional support and buoyancy.

- Encourage your dog to retrieve and fetch toys or objects in the water to engage their natural instincts and enhance their swimming skills. Start with short retrieves close to the shore and gradually increase the distance and difficulty as your dog's confidence and swimming abilities improve. Use positive reinforcement to reward your dog for successful retrieves and encourage them to enjoy the water.

- Prioritize water safety during swimming training sessions by supervising your dog closely at all times and ensuring they have a clear path to enter and exit the water. Monitor your dog's energy levels and body temperature, providing rest breaks and hydration as needed to prevent exhaustion and overheating. Familiarize yourself with common water hazards and safety precautions, such as currents, waves, and underwater obstacles, to keep your dog safe while swimming.

- Gradually progress your dog's swimming skills by introducing new challenges and environments, such as deeper water, rougher waves, or open water swimming. Provide plenty of opportunities for your dog to practice and build confidence in different swimming conditions, always prioritizing their safety and well-being.

What to Consider:

When swimming with dogs, it's important to observe some basic safety precautions to ensure that the experience is enjoyable and safe for both the dog and the owner. First and foremost, safety should be a priority by checking the swimming location for potential hazards such as strong currents, toxic plants, or wild animals. It's also advisable to adhere to water regulations and ensure that dogs swim in a suitable and permitted area.

Assessing your own dog's swimming abilities is important, and if necessary, using life jackets, especially for inexperienced swimmers or dogs unsure in the water, is recommended. Introducing your dog to water should be done slowly and gently to avoid overwhelming them. Throughout the swimming session, the dog should be constantly supervised to ensure they encounter no issues or danger.

Taking sufficient breaks to avoid exhaustion is advisable, as swimming can be demanding, especially for inexperienced dogs. After swimming, the dog should be thoroughly dried to prevent moisture in the fur and avoid potential skin problems, especially in the ears.

By observing these safety precautions, swimming with dogs can become an enjoyable and beneficial activity that not only improves the dog's physical fitness but also promotes their well-being.

At what age can I teach my puppy to swim?

Most dogs can start experiencing water at around 8 to 12 weeks of age, as long as it's done gently and under supervision. It's important to gradually and positively introduce the puppy to water by allowing them to play around the shore initially and then gradually showing them shallow water. Young puppies can tire quickly, so swimming sessions should be short and associated with plenty of praise and rewards to create a positive connection with water. However, swimming should only be fully introduced when the puppy has mastered the basics of walking and coordination and can move safely in the water.

What are signs that my dog is having trouble swimming and needs help?

- Swimming movements that appear uncoordinated or irregular
- A dog trying to keep its head above water and coughing or wheezing
- Increasing signs of exhaustion, such as slower swimming or a dog floating in the water and not making progress
- Panic or fear, which may manifest as excessive whining, howling, or thrashing

If you notice any of these signs, you should immediately bring your dog out of the water and ensure they are safe. If your dog shows signs of water inhalation or respiratory distress, seek veterinary help immediately.

What role does water quality play in my dog's safety when swimming?

Water quality plays a crucial role in your dog's safety when swimming. Contaminated water can contain potentially harmful bacteria, parasites, or chemical substances that could harm your dog. It's important to check the water quality before allowing your dog into the water and ensure it's safe for them. Avoid bodies of water with obvious pollution or signs of algae blooms, and pay attention to warnings or notices regarding water quality in your area. If you're unsure if the water is safe, it's best not to let your dog swim or look for alternatives.

How can I best dry my dog after swimming to prevent skin problems?

To prevent skin problems after swimming, it's important to thoroughly dry your dog to prevent moisture in the fur. Use a clean towel or a microfiber dryer to remove the water from the fur, focusing especially on areas such as the ears, between the toes, and under the belly where moisture can be trapped. If possible, use a hairdryer on a low setting to fully dry your dog's fur and avoid leaving them wet and unsupervised to prevent potential skin infection or irritation.

Rally Obedience

It combines elements of obedience and rally driving into an entertaining course characterized by teamwork, precision, and skill.

The Rally-Obedience course consists of a series of stations where various exercises must be performed. These exercises range from simple sit and down commands to more challenging maneuvers such as turns, jumps, and direction changes. Each station is marked with a sign indicating the exercise to be performed at that location, along with instructions guiding the team on how to execute the exercise.

During the course, the handler is allowed to support the dog with words, gestures, and hand signals to guide them through the exercises. It's about working together as a team and trusting each other.

Furthermore, Rally Obedience provides an excellent opportunity to improve the physical and mental fitness of the dog. The course requires agility, coordination, and endurance, which serve as good physical exercise for both the dog and the handler. Additionally, completing the various exercises contributes to the mental stimulation of the dog, helping them reach their full potential.

For dog owners interested in Rally Obedience, there are some important tips to consider. Firstly, it's important that both the dog and the handler have basic obedience skills before starting training. This makes it easier for the team to master the exercises in the course and be successful.

Additionally, it's advisable to start with simple exercises and gradually increase the difficulty as the dog progresses. This helps the dog build confidence and experience success, which in turn boosts their motivation.

Step by Step Introduction:

- Introduce your dog to the various rally signs used in competitions, which typically indicate specific behaviors or exercises to be performed at each station. Start by familiarizing your dog with the signs individually, using treats and praise to create a positive association. Gradually incorporate multiple signs into training sessions to simulate the flow of a rally course.
- Focus on perfecting your dog's heelwork and positioning during rally obedience exercises. Practice walking together in a precise heel position, with your dog positioned at your side and paying attention to your movements. Use verbal cues and hand signals to guide your dog's position and reinforce good heelwork behavior.
- Train your dog to perform specific obedience exercises at each rally station, such as sits, downs, turns, and recalls. Use positive reinforcement techniques such as treats, praise, and toys to reward your dog for successfully completing each exercise. Practice transitioning smoothly between stations and maintaining focus and attention throughout the course.
- Develop your dog's focus and engagement during rally obedience training by incorporating attention-building exercises into your training routine. Practice maintaining eye contact and responsiveness to your cues, even in distracting environments or amidst other dogs. Use high-value rewards and interactive play to reinforce your dog's focus and enthusiasm for training.
- As your dog becomes more proficient in individual rally exercises, start stringing them together into full rally courses. Set up mock courses in different locations, using

rally signs or makeshift markers to indicate each station. Practice navigating the course with your dog, focusing on smooth transitions, accurate execution of exercises, and maintaining a positive and confident attitude throughout the run.

- Prepare for rally obedience competitions by simulating competition conditions during training sessions. Practice in a variety of environments and distractions, gradually increasing the level of difficulty to mimic the challenges of a real competition. Focus on building confidence and teamwork with your dog, and remember to have fun and enjoy the experience together.

- Rally obedience is a dynamic and evolving sport that offers endless opportunities for learning and improvement. Embrace each training session as an opportunity to strengthen your bond with your dog and celebrate your progress together.

Can every dog do Rally Obedience?

Rally Obedience is suitable for dogs of all sizes, and ages. However, it's important to ensure that your dog is healthy and has basic obedience skills before starting training. Older dogs can also participate in Rally Obedience as long as they are physically capable. It's important to adapt the training to your dog's individual needs and abilities to ensure that they are successful and enjoy the training.

Are there different difficulty levels in Rally Obedience?

Yes, Rally Obedience offers various difficulty levels ranging from beginner to advanced. Beginner exercises typically involve simple turns, direction changes, and basic obedience exercises, while advanced exercises may include more complex maneuvers such as jumps, slalom courses, and backing up. It's important to adjust the difficulty level to match your dog's skills and gradually increase it to ensure they are successful and enjoy the training.

Can I train Rally Obedience at home?
Yes, many of the exercises can be trained at home to improve their skills. You can set up your own mini-course and regularly train with your dog to teach them the various exercises. It's important to create a calm and undisturbed environment so your dog can fully focus on the training. By training regularly at home, you can track your dog's progress and work on their weaknesses.

Are there specific mistakes I should avoid when training Rally Obedience?
A common mistake in Rally Obedience training is to progress too quickly and overwhelm the dog. Start with simple exercises and take it slowly to ensure your dog understands and performs them correctly.

How can I maintain my dog's motivation during Rally Obedience training?
Maintaining your dog's motivation during Rally Obedience training is crucial for success. Keep the training varied and interesting by incorporating different exercises and challenges. It's also important to keep training sessions short to prevent your dog from getting bored or overwhelmed. If your dog enjoys the training and feels rewarded, they will be motivated to continue giving their best.

What should I do if my dog gets distracted during the course?
Distractions during the course can be challenging, but they also provide an opportunity to improve your dog's skills. If

122

your dog gets distracted during the course, try to regain their attention by interacting with them and encouraging them to focus on you. Use positive reinforcement to reward their behavior when they focus on you, and gradually work on improving their ability to stay focused even amidst distractions. Through patient training, you can help your dog cope with distractions and successfully complete the course.

Can Rally Obedience help my dog solve behavior problems?

Yes, Rally Obedience can help solve behavior problems such as disobedience or attention deficits by strengthening the bond between dog and handler and mentally and physically stimulating the dog. Through regular training and positive reinforcement, you can help your dog improve their skills and correct their behavior. Rally Obedience offers your dog a structured and fun way to channel their energy and use their natural instincts, leading to a happier and more balanced dog.

How can I make my dog faster and more efficient in completing the course?

Work on the speed and precision of the exercises by gradually increasing the difficulty of training and giving your dog clear signals. Praise them when they perform the exercises quickly and correctly to increase their motivation. It can also be helpful to work on your dog's endurance and conditioning to improve their performance and speed. Through targeted training, you can improve your dog's skills and make them more efficient in completing the course.

Agility

Agility training for dogs is much more than just a physical activity. It's a holistic activity that promotes both physical and mental health. By overcoming various obstacles like hurdles, tunnels, and weave poles, dogs learn to follow instructions, focus on the course, and make quick decisions while navigating obstacles.

Agility training can have a positive impact on dogs' behavior and abilities in various everyday situations. Here are some examples:

Obedience and control: Through agility training, dogs learn to respond to commands and follow their owner's instructions. This obedience and control can pay off in everyday situations such as walks, encounters with other dogs, or entering rooms. A dog that has learned to listen to its owner is less likely to exhibit unwanted behavior or get into dangerous situations.

Coordination and agility: The improved coordination and agility that dogs develop through agility training can manifest in various situations, such as navigating tight spaces or uneven terrain during a walk. A dog that has learned to effectively control its body and overcome obstacles will be overall more adept and secure in its movement.

Self-confidence and self-control: Dogs that regularly engage in agility training often develop increased self-confidence and better self-control. This can manifest in situations such as dealing with new environments, meeting unfamiliar people or animals, or coping with unfamiliar stimuli. A confident dog will be less anxious or uncertain and better able to face new challenges.

Physical fitness and endurance: The improved physical fitness and endurance that dogs develop through agility training can manifest in many aspects of daily life. For example, a fitter dog will have more energy for long walks or playtimes and be less prone to injuries or illnesses.

Step by Step Introduction:

- Start by introducing your dog to agility equipment one piece at a time. Begin with simple obstacles like low jumps or tunnels. Use positive reinforcement techniques such as treats, praise, and toys to encourage your dog to explore and interact with the equipment.
- Focus on building a strong foundation of key agility skills. Teach your dog to follow your directional cues, such as left, right, and forward, using verbal commands and body language. Practice basic maneuvers like sending your dog over jumps or through tunnels on command.
- Weave poles are one of the most challenging agility obstacles for dogs to master. Start by using a set of spaced-out poles and guiding your dog through them with treats or toys. Gradually decrease the distance between the poles as your dog becomes more proficient, eventually transitioning to standard weave pole spacing.
- Proper jumping technique is crucial for agility success and injury prevention. Teach your dog to jump with good form,

clearing obstacles cleanly without knocking bars. Start with low jumps and gradually increase the height as your dog's confidence and skill level improve.

- Contact obstacles like the A-frame and seesaw require dogs to make contact with designated zones to complete the obstacle safely. Train your dog to navigate these obstacles with precision, ensuring they touch the contact zones with their paws for consistent performance.
- Once your dog has mastered individual agility skills, begin stringing them together into sequences and courses. Start with simple combinations and gradually increase the complexity as your dog becomes more proficient. Focus on maintaining clear communication and reinforcing desired behaviors throughout the course.
- Agility training is a continuous process that requires regular practice and consistency. Set aside dedicated training sessions each week to work on agility skills with your dog. Celebrate progress and remain patient during setbacks, always prioritizing your dog's enjoyment and well-being.

When practicing the sport of agility, there are certain aspects that should be avoided:

To ensure the well-being and safety of the dog during agility training, certain aspects should be considered. Overtraining and overexertion should be avoided by appropriately dosing the training and scheduling rest periods. Both the obstacles and the dog's equipment should be safe and appropriate to avoid injuries.

The jump height of the obstacles should correspond to the dog's skill level and size to prevent overexertion. It is important not to overwhelm or overtrain the dog, but rather to motivate them with patience and positive reinforcement. Additionally, always pay attention to the dog's health by examining signs of illness or injury before training or competition, and adjust or interrupt the training if they are feeling unwell.

By considering these points, the safety and well-being of the dog during agility training can be ensured.

Problems

Boxers are captivating companions, brimming with energy, affection, and individuality. Yet, at times, their actions, though perplexing to us, can lead to friction and misconceptions.

Behavioral challenges in Boxers span a spectrum, ranging from mild to severe. Excessive barking, aggression towards humans or fellow animals, indoor accidents, and object destruction are among the hurdles dog owners may encounter.

The initial stride in tackling behavioral issues in Boxers is comprehension. These behaviors often serve as expressions of needs, anxieties, or even underlying health conditions. Delving into the motivations behind these actions enables us to devise tailored solutions that not only alleviate symptoms but also target the root causes.

For instance, incessant barking may stem from feelings of loneliness, excitement, or territorial instincts. Aggression might signal fear, insecurity, or insufficient socialization. Indoor accidents could indicate stress, fear, or health issues, while object destruction may result from boredom, separation anxiety, or lack of mental stimulation.

By gaining deeper insights into the needs, fears, and personalities of our Boxers, we can formulate more precise and impactful remedies. This often entails a blend of patience, empathy, and innovative strategies aimed at positively shaping our dog's conduct.

In the forthcoming sections, we will navigate through various behavioral issues in Boxers, dissecting their potential origins and offering pragmatic solutions for each facet of these dilemmas. Additionally, we will delve into diverse training techniques, behavioral therapies, and methods of behavior modification to foster a more harmonious and enriching coexistence with our Boxers.

The path to addressing behavioral challenges in Boxers may pose its challenges, yet it is ultimately gratifying. By endeavoring to comprehend the needs and behaviors of our Boxers and responding aptly, we can not only enhance their quality of life but also deepen the bond we share with them.

Aggression

Aggression is a complex behavior pattern in dogs that can take on various forms and often has underlying causes. It's important to understand that aggression is a normal behavior that can occur in dogs in certain situations, but it becomes problematic when it's uncontrolled or inappropriate. There are different types of aggression in dogs, including territorial aggression, aggressive behavior towards other dogs or animals, aggressive behavior towards humans, and fear aggression. Each form of aggression may have different causes and requires an individual approach to training and behavior modification.

Boxers are generally friendly and loyal dogs, but they can display aggression if not properly socialized or trained.

Territorial Aggression

Territorial aggression in dogs is a behavioral problem that can occur in many dogs and is often influenced by various factors. This form of aggression occurs when a dog defends its territory or the area it considers its own. It can lead to undesirable behaviors such as barking, growling, attacks, and even biting.

This behavior is often deeply rooted in the instincts and genetics of dogs. Their ancestors, the wolves, defended their territories against intruders to secure resources and ensure their survival.

Additionally, resource guarding may play a role in territorial aggression. Dogs may exhibit aggressive behavior to defend food, toys, or a sleeping area. This can occur especially in dogs living in multi-dog households or those that have experienced resource scarcity.

Fear and insecurity are also factors that can contribute to territorial aggression in dogs. An insecure dog may aggressively defend its territory to ward off potential threats and feel safe.

Aggressive Behavior Towards Other Dogs

A fundamental factor contributing to aggression between dogs lies in their natural social structure. Dogs are inherently social animals that tend to live in groups and establish a hierarchy or dominance structure. Within this hierarchy, there are dominant and submissive individuals. Aggression can occur when a dog tries to establish or defend its dominance over another dog. This may occur during encounters at the park, while playing, or even within the home when two dogs compete for their owner's attention.

To deepen these concepts, let's consider some examples from dogs' daily lives. Imagine a situation at the park where one dog finds a ball and starts playing with it. Another dog, also fond of ball games, tries to grab the ball. If the first dog feels that its toy is threatened, it may exhibit aggressive behavior to defend it. A similar scenario could unfold at home when a dog defends its food, especially if it has previously experienced resource scarcity.

Another important aspect is the role of the owner in the development and management of aggressive behavior in dogs. The way the owner interacts with their dog, reads its signals, and responds to them can have a significant impact on how the dog reacts to other dogs. An owner who shows insecurity or fear when their dog encounters other dogs may contribute to the dog behaving similarly, leading to aggressive behavior. Furthermore, environmental factors such as stress, overstimulation, or territorial behavior can increase the likelihood of aggressive behavior between dogs. In crowded or noisy environments, dogs may feel threatened or stressed, reducing their tolerance threshold for conflicts.

Aggressive Behavior Towards Humans

There are various reasons why dogs may exhibit aggressive behavior towards humans. One of them is fear and insecurity. Dogs that have not been adequately socialized, for example, those raised in shelters or rescue facilities, may perceive humans as a threat and react aggressively when approached by them. These dogs may not have experienced enough positive human interactions to build trust.

Previous traumatic experiences can also play a role. A dog that has been abused or neglected in the past may develop aggressive behavior as a protective mechanism. For example, a dog that has experienced violence may automatically associate humans with pain and mistreatment and therefore react aggressively to defend itself.

The way a dog is raised and treated also has a significant impact on its behavior towards humans. Dogs that are treated roughly or violently may learn to perceive humans as a threat and react aggressively to defend themselves.

Fear Aggression

A common form of fear aggression is social fear aggression, where a dog reacts anxiously or aggressively in the presence of other dogs or humans. This can occur in dogs that have not been properly socialized or have had negative experiences in the past, such as attacks by other dogs or inappropriate behavior from humans. An example would be a dog that reacts aggressively to other dogs due to a bad past experience, growling or snapping when they approach.

There is also situational fear aggression, which occurs in specific situations or environments that trigger fear or stress in the dog. An example would be a dog that reacts anxiously and aggressively when taken to the veterinarian or when placed in a crowded or noisy environment.

Physical Signs of Aggression in Dogs

- You can recognize aggression in your dog by certain physical characteristics. An aggressive dog may curl its lips, bare its teeth, and pull back its eyelids tightly. The eyes may have a fixed stare.
- An aggressive dog may assume an upright and stiff body posture. Its body may be tense, with a raised head and erect ears.
- The fur of an aggressive dog may stand up, especially on the back and neck, making it appear larger.
- A growling dog signals that it feels uncomfortable or threatened and is ready to defend itself.
- An aggressive dog may show its teeth to threaten or warn.
- An aggressive dog may stare at other animals or humans without looking away.

Minimizing Aggression:

An important step is early socialization of your dog. Even in puppyhood, you should ensure that your dog has positive experiences with other dogs. This can be achieved through controlled interactions in safe environments, where they learn to appropriately respond to other dogs and develop social skills.

Another crucial aspect is training and obedience of your dog. A well-trained dog is less prone to aggressive behavior, as it listens to your commands and is more controllable in stressful situations.

A dog that reacts aggressively when strangers enter the house can learn through targeted training to remain calm and have positive interactions with visitors. This can be achieved through gradual training, where the dog is initially kept at a distance and then gradually introduced closer to the visitors while receiving positive reinforcement for calm behavior.

It is also important that you, as a dog owner, avoid potentially conflict-prone situations or appropriately control your dog in such situations. Keep your dog on a leash if necessary or bring them to areas where they have less stress and are less exposed to sensory overload.

Territorial behavior in the garden or backyard can be controlled by establishing clear boundaries and rules for the dog. For example, specific areas can be defined where the dog can play or stay, while other areas are off-limits, especially when passersby or neighbors are nearby.

Observe your dog's behavior closely, especially around other dogs. Learn to interpret their body language to recognize signs of discomfort, fear, or aggression early on. This way, you can potentially identify conflict-prone situations in time and respond appropriately to avoid escalations.

Positive reinforcement plays a crucial role in promoting desired behavior. Praise and reward your dog when they display calm and appropriate behavior, especially in territorial situations. This can help reinforce the behavior you want to promote.

It is important to emphasize that aggression in dogs is a serious problem that should not be ignored. Early intervention and professional help can help modify aggressive behavior and ensure the safety and well-being of your dog as well as other people and animals. By gaining a deeper understanding of the causes and triggers of aggression, we can contribute to improving the quality of life of our dogs and creating a safer environment for everyone.

Fear

Fear in dogs is a widespread phenomenon influenced by various causes and triggers. Similar to humans, fear in dogs can take on different forms and affect their behavior, health, and quality of life. Understanding the different types of fears in dogs is important to respond appropriately and help them cope with their fears.

Boxers can be sensitive dogs and may develop fearfulness if not exposed to a wide range of stimuli during their critical socialization period, which typically occurs between 3 and 14 weeks of age.

One common form of fear in dogs is separation anxiety. Dogs are naturally social animals and can experience anxiety when left alone. This can lead to undesirable behaviors such as excessive barking, destruction of objects, or even uncontrollable urination. An example is a dog that starts whining and howling as soon as its owner leaves the house. This behavior can be mitigated through appropriate training methods and possibly by introducing distractions or comfort items such as toys or chew treats.

Another common form of fear in dogs is fear of loud noises, such as fireworks, thunderstorms, or even loud traffic noise. Dogs may react anxiously to such noises and hide, tremble, or try to escape. In such cases, it can be helpful to set up a quiet and safe retreat for the dog to provide security and comfort.

Additionally, dogs can also develop specific fears related to traumatic experiences or negative past experiences. An example is a dog that was attacked by another dog and has since been afraid of other dogs. In such cases, it is important to be patient and help the dog gradually rebuild its trust.

It is also important to note that fear in dogs is not always obvious and can manifest in various behaviors. For example, some dogs may react aggressively when they are fearful, while others may withdraw and become passive. Therefore, it is important to recognize the individual signals and expressions of a dog and respond appropriately.

An Overview of Additional Potential Triggers:

- Some dogs may be fearful or distrustful of strangers, especially if they have not been properly socialized or have had negative experiences with people.
- Visiting the veterinarian can be stressful for many dogs, as it may involve unpleasant experiences such as examinations, injections, or even surgeries.
- A sudden change in environment, such as moving or traveling, can trigger fear in dogs as they find themselves in an unfamiliar and unfamiliar situation.
- Dogs may react anxiously to other animals, especially when conflicts or aggressions arise, whether with other dogs, cats, or wild animals.
- Objects that are new or unusual to the dog, such as large machinery, oddly shaped objects, or even simple household items, can trigger fear as they may be perceived as potential threats.
- Dogs are often creatures of habit and may react anxiously to changes in their daily routine, whether it's a new schedule, new people in the household, or changes in feeding or grooming.
- In addition to separation anxiety, some dogs may also fear being left alone, even if they don't necessarily suffer from separation anxiety. The feeling of isolation can cause fear and stress in some dogs.

- New and unfamiliar smells can trigger fear or discomfort in dogs as they may be interpreted as potential danger. This is particularly relevant in situations such as visiting new places or entering unfamiliar homes.
- In addition to loud noises, unfamiliar or strange sounds, such as sudden knocking noises or the rustling of wind, can trigger fear in dogs as they may not know what is causing them.
- Some dogs may react anxiously to certain types of touches or manipulations, whether it's wearing collars or harnesses, brushing their fur, or examining certain parts of their body.

Minimizing Fear:

Fear in dogs is a widespread problem that can have various causes. Some dogs are naturally more fearful, while others develop fearful behavior due to traumatic experiences or lack of socialization. Regardless of the cause, it's important to take your dog's fear seriously and help them feel safer and more relaxed.

The first step in addressing your dog's fear is patience. It's important to recognize that it takes time to gain your dog's trust and overcome their fears. Don't push your dog into situations that might frighten them; instead, give them the opportunity to gradually acclimate to new environments, people, and animals.

Positive reinforcement is an effective way to influence your dog's behavior. Reward calm and relaxed behavior with praise, treats, or toys to create positive associations with new situations. This way, your dog will learn that it's safe to relax in their surroundings.

Socialization is another important aspect of addressing your dog's fear. Introduce them gently to new people, animals, and environments, ensuring that these encounters are positive and stress-free. This will help strengthen your dog's confidence and assist them in overcoming their fears.

Training is also crucial in alleviating your dog's fear. Train them in basic obedience commands such as "sit," "down," and "stay" to provide them with security and help them calm down in stressful situations. Through regular training, your dog will learn to pay attention to your commands and feel more secure.

Relaxation techniques such as gentle massage or practicing calm breathing can also help alleviate your dog's fear and assist them in calming down when they're anxious.

It's important to emphasize that punishment is never an appropriate response to fearful behavior. Never punish your dog for their fears, as this can intensify their fear and damage the trust between you.

If your dog's fear is severe or affecting their daily life, seek professional help. A veterinarian or behavior consultant can provide individual advice and solutions for your dog's specific needs.

What are the effects of untreated anxiety in dogs?
Untreated anxiety in dogs can lead to a variety of problems. Firstly, behavioral issues may arise, including aggression, inappropriate elimination, and property destruction. Anxiety can also lead to health problems as it causes stress, which can weaken the immune system. Long-term stress can lead to increased susceptibility to illness and diminish the dog's quality of life. Additionally, untreated anxiety can worsen the relationship between the dog and the owner, as the dog may develop trust issues or exhibit undesirable behavior, leading to frustration on the owner's part.

Can anxiety in dogs be genetically predisposed?
Yes, anxiety in dogs can be genetically predisposed. Studies have shown that certain genetic traits may be associated with a higher risk of anxiety disorders in dogs. These genetic factors can influence the dog's response to stress and its ability to cope with new or unfamiliar situations. It's important to note that while genetic predispositions may play a role, environmental and socialization factors also have a significant impact on a dog's anxiety behavior.

Chewing

Dogs chew for various reasons. This behavior often stems from the instinctive need to chew, inherited from their wild ancestors. Chewing originally served to grind food and clean teeth. Even domesticated dogs often retain this instinct and enjoy chewing on various objects.

Boxers have strong jaws and a natural inclination to chew, which can lead to destructive behavior if not managed properly.

Furthermore, chewing can also serve to clean and strengthen teeth. Chewing on bones or specialized chew toys can remove plaque and massage the gums, contributing to dental health.

Boredom can be another reason for chewing. Dogs that lack sufficient mental and physical stimulation often resort to chewing to occupy themselves. This can lead to destructive behavior if suitable alternatives are not provided.

Additionally, dogs may chew out of stress or anxiety. Similar to humans who bite their nails or play with objects to calm themselves, dogs may use chewing as a coping mechanism when feeling uneasy.

To manage your dog's chewing, it's important to provide them with sufficient appropriate toys to chew on. This can help satisfy their chewing instincts and provide them with a healthy outlet for keeping busy. Additionally, ensure your dog receives enough mental and physical stimulation to avoid boredom. Regular walks, playtime, and involvement in activities can help keep your dog happy and balanced.

Triggers for Chewing:

- When a dog doesn't receive enough mental and physical stimulation, it may resort to chewing to keep itself occupied.
- Dogs have a natural inclination to chew, inherited from their wild ancestors. This can lead them to chew on various objects.
- Chewing on bones or specialized chew toys can serve to clean and strengthen teeth.
- Dogs may use chewing as a coping mechanism when feeling stressed or anxious.
- Dogs may chew in the absence of their owners, especially if they suffer from separation anxiety.
- In some cases, chewing may be attributed to hormonal changes, such as during puberty or when a female dog is in heat.
- A lack of certain nutrients in the diet may lead a dog to chew more to compensate for this deficiency.
- Sometimes, chronic pain or discomfort from an underlying illness can cause a dog to chew more to distract or soothe itself.
- Some dogs may chew out of curiosity about new objects or materials they discover.
- If a dog hasn't been properly trained to understand which objects it's allowed to chew on and which it's not, this can lead to undesirable chewing.

Minimizing Chewing:

To minimize your dog's chewing, there are various effective approaches. An important step is providing appropriate chew toys specifically designed for dogs that are safe and durable. This allows you to satisfy your dog's natural chewing behavior without it chewing on undesirable objects.

Additionally, it's crucial to provide your dog with ample exercise and mental stimulation. Regular walks, playtime, and obedience training help ensure your dog is adequately stimulated and less likely to chew out of boredom.

During training, it's important to monitor your dog and interrupt unwanted chewing. Redirect them to approved alternatives and reward them when they do the right thing. Positive reinforcement is an effective means of promoting desired behavior.

If your dog chews due to stress or anxiety, consider relaxation and calming techniques such as regular quiet times or training focused on building trust and security.

A balanced diet meeting your dog's nutritional needs can also help reduce the urge to chew due to nutrient deficiencies.

Remember to use chewing as a reward as well, giving your dog a chew toy when they exhibit desired behavior. This reinforces positive behavior and channels their chewing in an acceptable manner.

What types of chew toys are best for dogs?
Popular options include sturdy rubber toys like Kong toys, which can help satisfy the dog's chewing instincts while also cleaning its teeth. Nylon or rubber bones are also a good choice as they are durable and appeal to the dog's chewing instinct without the risk of splintering or breaking. Interactive chew toys that hide treats or food can help mentally engage the dog and promote its chewing behavior.

Nipping

Nipping behavior in dogs, the quick snapping or biting at hands, clothing, or other objects, can have various causes often rooted in their natural behavior and communication. One of the most common motives is play behavior. Dogs often interact with each other by chasing, snapping, and roughhousing. So, if your dog tries to catch your hand or clothing, it could simply be attempting to play with you in a similar way as it would with other dogs.

Boxer puppies, like many other breeds, may nip during play or when excited.

Excessive excitement can also lead to nipping. When a dog is overstimulated, whether it's due to joyful anticipation, excitement over a new visitor, or other stimuli, it may have difficulty controlling its emotions. Nipping could then serve as an outlet for this excess energy.

Additionally, nipping can be an expression of insecurity or fear. If a dog feels threatened or uncomfortable, it may try to ward off potential dangers by snapping. This could be a defensive reaction to protect itself or drive away the perceived threat.

Another factor that can lead to nipping is overstimulation. Dogs perceive their environment through their senses, and when faced with too many new impressions or an overwhelming situation, they may react with stress or anxiety. Nipping could then be a way to cope with this sensory overload.

Finally, a lack of sufficient physical and mental stimulation can lead dogs to become bored and exhibit undesirable behavior, including nipping. Dogs are naturally active animals, and if they don't receive enough exercise or mental stimulation, they may try to discharge their energy in other ways.

Triggers of Nipping:
- Dogs tend to snap at things while playing, similar to how they would with other dogs.
- When a dog is overstimulated, whether through play, excitement over visitors, or other thrilling events, it may tend to nip.
- Dogs may snap to defend themselves or to ward off a perceived threat when feeling uncertain or fearful.
- Too many new impressions or an overwhelming environment can cause a dog to feel stressed and exhibit nipping as a response.
- A lack of sufficient physical and mental stimulation can lead dogs to become bored and display destructive behavior like nipping.
- Sometimes, nipping is unintentionally reinforced through reward or lack of correction during puppyhood and then persists as a habit.
- In some cases, hormonal imbalance, such as during adolescence or certain health issues, can lead to unwanted nipping.
- Dogs not adequately accustomed to various situations and people may feel insecure and exhibit nipping as a response to new or unfamiliar stimuli.
- Dogs may snap when experiencing pain or discomfort to signal that something is wrong.
- In certain cases, nipping can be a form of territorial behavior, especially when the dog feels threatened or wants to defend its territory.

Why Dogs Should Not Nip:

It's important to teach your dog not to nip. Even though this behavior may be natural, it poses potential risks such as accidental injuries and social discomfort. By suppressing this behavior, you promote the safety and well-being of your family as well as positive social interaction of your dog with others. Additionally, it strengthens your dog's obedience and respect toward you as the owner and lays the foundation for comprehensive training. Methods like positive reinforcement, distraction with toys, and clear communication about undesirable behavior are effective ways to teach your dog not to nip.

Minimizing Nipping:

To minimize nipping behavior in your dog, there are various effective methods you can apply. An important approach is positive reinforcement. Reward your dog with praise and treats when he exhibits appropriate behavior, such as playing calmly without nipping. At the same time, it's important to provide your dog with alternative outlets for activity. Offer him toys to chew on or tug at, and immediately redirect him if he attempts to nip at you. Clear communication also plays an important role. Use a firm "No" or other interruption to signal that nipping is unwanted.

Additionally, it may be helpful to interrupt play for a short period if your dog tends to nip. This gives him the opportunity to calm down and understand that nipping leads to the end of the game. Regular training of basic obedience commands like "Sit," "Down," or "Stay" can also help minimize nipping behavior.

It's also important to ensure that your dog receives sufficient exercise and mental stimulation. Walks, outdoor playtimes, and puzzle games can channel his energy and reduce boredom, which in turn can minimize nipping behavior. Additionally, avoid overstimulating your dog or putting him in stressful situations to promote his well-being.

Jumping

The behavior of jumping in dogs can be attributed to various reasons. Furthermore, jumping can be a way for your dog to express its joy and excitement, whether it's greeting its owners, meeting other dogs, or anticipating activities like walks or games. Another reason for jumping may be that the dog wants to attract attention.

Boxers are enthusiastic dogs and may jump on people as a form of greeting or excitement.

Dogs are intelligent animals and have learned that jumping is an effective way to get attention. If they jump and receive the desired reaction - whether it's praise, petting, or even negative attention like scolding - they are likely to repeat this behavior to get what they want. Sometimes, jumping can also be a way for your dog to release excess energy, especially if it has been alone for a long time or hasn't had enough exercise.

Upon reuniting with you, it may want to discharge by jumping. Another possible reason for jumping is a lack of training. If your dog was allowed to jump as a puppy and was never corrected, it may have never learned that this behavior is inappropriate. By understanding the reasons why your dog jumps, you can take more targeted measures to correct the behavior and provide alternative ways for it to express its needs.

Triggers for jumping:

Greeting: When you come home after a long day and your dog is excited with anticipation and joy over your return, he may possibly jump up and down in front of you to express his excitement.

Play invitation: When you're playing with your dog outside in the park and he suddenly spots a fellow canine companion he'd like to play with, he might jump up and down with excitement at the prospect of playing with the other dog.

Anticipation of an activity: Before going for a walk with your dog and you grab the leash, he might jump up and down with excitement about the upcoming walk time.

Uncertainty or fear: When you take your dog for the first time to a new environment, such as a bustling marketplace, he might jump up and down in front of you out of uncertainty or fear of the new sounds and crowds, seeking your closeness.

Begging for attention: When you're sitting at the dining table eating something, your dog might jump up and down in front of you to get your attention and hope that you'll share some of your food with him.

Exuberant reaction: When you come home after a long day and enthusiastically greet your dog, he might be excited by your energy and enthusiasm over your return, jumping up and down in front of you to mirror your mood.

Minimizing Jumping:

To minimize the undesirable behavior of jumping in your dog, there are several effective approaches. First and foremost, it's important not to reward jumping by not giving your dog attention when he attempts to jump. Instead, you can ignore him until he calms down and keeps all four paws on the ground. Once he's calm, you can praise or reward him to reinforce the desired behavior.

Another important step is to offer your dog alternative behaviors. This means teaching him to sit or lie down when he's excited instead of jumping. Positively reward and reinforce these calm behaviors to solidify them.

Regular training sessions are also crucial for promoting the desired behavior. Practice sitting or lying down with your dog in various situations and reward him for remaining calm. Be consistent in your behavior and also encourage other family members and visitors to adhere to the same rules to avoid confusion and reinforce the desired behavior.

When greeting your dog with visitors or in other exciting situations, distraction can be an effective method to minimize jumping. Use toys or treats to distract your dog and prevent him from jumping.

Finally, you can also apply conditioned negative reinforcement to discourage jumping. This means making an unpleasant noise or creating an uncomfortable sensation when your dog attempts to jump. However, sensitivity and caution are required to avoid scaring or confusing your dog.

What alternatives to jumping could dogs learn?

Dogs can learn various alternative behaviors to express their excitement and joy without jumping. These include sitting, giving paw, lying down, or maintaining calm behavior while approaching their owner. By learning alternative behaviors, dogs can learn to exhibit appropriate behavior when greeting people.

How can guests be encouraged not to reinforce dogs' jumping?

It's important to educate guests on how to behave when greeted by the dog to avoid reinforcing jumping. They should be instructed to ignore the dog until it calms down and not to encourage the behavior by reacting to it. Instead, they can be encouraged to remain calm and only interact with the dog when it displays appropriate behavior, such as sitting or standing calmly.

Whining

Dogs communicate with us in various ways, and whining is one of their most common forms of expression. It's important to understand that dogs whine to express different needs or emotions.

Boxers may whine to communicate various needs or desires, such as attention, food, or the need to go outside.

One common reason for dogs whining is to request attention or help. When a dog is hungry, needs to go outside, or simply seeks companionship, it may try to attract its owner's attention by whining. For example, a dog with empty food bowls may whine in hopes of getting food, or a puppy feeling lonely may whine to call for its family.

Whining can also be a sign of discomfort or pain. Dogs cannot verbalize when they feel unwell, but they can indicate that something is wrong through whining. For instance, if a dog is sick or injured, it may try to alert its owners that it needs help by whining.

Sometimes a dog's whining may also indicate emotional needs. Dogs can feel anxious, stressed, or frustrated, and whining can be an expression of these feelings. For example, a dog suffering from separation anxiety may whine when its owner leaves the house. Likewise, a dog in an unfamiliar or frightening situation may whine to ask for support from its owners.

It's important to consider a dog's whining in context and identify potential causes. By observing the dog's behavior and taking its environment into account, dog owners can better understand why their dog is whining and respond appropriately, whether it's by fulfilling its needs, providing comfort in stressful situations, or seeking veterinary help for pain or discomfort.

Additional triggers:

- Hunger, thirst, the need for a walk, toilet needs, or the desire for attention and companionship can cause a dog to whine.

- When a dog is in pain, whether it's due to an injury, illness, or other health issue, it may try to draw attention to it by whining. For example, joint pain, stomach problems, or dental issues can cause a dog to whine.

- Dogs can experience fear or stress in various situations, whether it's due to loud noises, unfamiliar environments, separation anxiety, or other stressful events. Whining can be an expression of this emotional distress.

- If a dog is under-stimulated or doesn't receive enough mental and physical stimulation, it may express its dissatisfaction or boredom through whining. Similarly, frustration over unmet needs or misunderstanding of certain rules or restrictions can lead to whining.

- Some dogs tend to whine out of joy or excitement, especially when looking forward to something, such as before receiving their favorite toy or when greeting someone they like.

- Dogs can also communicate with other dogs or humans through whining, whether it's to request play, express fear, or seek support.

Should Whining be Minimized:

A dog's whining is often an expression of its needs, emotions, or attempts at communication. Whether one should try to minimize whining depends on various factors.

In some cases, whining is a natural part of a dog's communication and can be an important way to draw attention to needs or issues. For example, if a dog is in pain or feeling unwell, whining is often an indication that medical help is needed. In such situations, it's important to identify the cause of the whining and respond appropriately, rather than simply suppressing the whining.

On the other hand, excessive or inappropriate whining can also be a sign that the dog has unmet needs or that its behavior needs to be corrected through training. In such cases, it may be sensible to develop strategies to minimize or modify the whining to promote a more harmonious living environment.

Minimizing Whining:

Minimizing a dog's whining requires a compassionate approach and targeted measures to understand and address the underlying causes of the behavior. Firstly, it's important to ensure that the dog's basic needs are met, such as regular feeding, ample water, adequate exercise and mental stimulation, as well as sufficient social interaction and attention.

Training plays a crucial role in teaching your dog alternative behaviors and showing it how to express its needs in acceptable ways. Through positive reinforcement, praise, and treats when the dog exhibits calm behavior, you can encourage it to reduce whining.

Creating a calm and relaxed environment for your dog, especially in stressful situations, is important. This can be achieved through gentle touch, soothing music, or specific relaxation techniques for dogs. If your dog's whining could be attributed to pain or health issues, a veterinary examination is essential to identify the cause and initiate appropriate treatments.

Fear and stress can also be causes of whining. Identify potential triggers and look for ways to minimize or avoid them. This may involve changes in the environment, desensitization training, or the use of calming aids.

How to Distinguish Between Different Types of Whining in Dogs:

The whining of dogs can have different meanings depending on the context and tone. A deep, moaning whine often indicates pain or discomfort, while a short and cheerful-sounding whine is more likely an expression of excitement or joy. An anxious whine may manifest as a trembling or high-pitched whine, while a whining sound associated with toys or other dogs often indicates a desire for interaction. It's important to interpret whining in the context of the situation and the dog's behavior to better understand its needs or emotions.

Howling

Dogs are fascinating animals, and their behavior, including howling, is often complex and multifaceted. The howling of dogs has various reasons and functions, ranging from social interactions to emotional states.

Boxers may howl in response to sirens, other loud noises, or if they are anxious or seeking attention.

One of the most common reasons why dogs howl is for social communication. In the wild, dogs can reach other members of their pack over long distances through howling. This can serve to announce their presence, coordinate group members, or simply seek contact. Even in domestic settings, dogs may howl to signal their presence or to attract the attention of other dogs or humans.

Furthermore, dogs sometimes respond to specific sounds with howling. For example, they may respond to the howling of sirens, the rumble of engines, or even music with their own howling. This could be because such sounds contain certain frequencies that appeal to dogs and prompt them to respond with similar sounds.

Emotional states also play a role in dogs' howling. Loneliness is a common trigger, especially when a dog is left alone for extended periods. In such cases, howling can be a way to express their feelings of separation or isolation. Anxious dogs may also howl to communicate their restlessness or fear, whether it's due to loud noises, unfamiliar environments, or other stressors.

It's important to note that dogs' howling is a natural behavior deeply rooted in their evolutionary history. It serves various purposes and can have different meanings depending on the context and the individual dog. While some dogs may tend to howl more frequently, others may do so less often. Ultimately, howling is part of the diverse communication repertoire of dogs, allowing them to connect with their environment and other individuals.

Should Howling be Minimized:

The howling of dogs is a natural part of their behavioral repertoire and can have various meanings depending on the context. In most cases, it is not necessary or advisable to minimize a dog's howling, as it often serves an important function, whether as social communication, a reaction to environmental stimuli, or an expression of emotions.

However, there are situations where excessive howling may be undesirable, especially if it becomes a problem for the people in the vicinity or for the dog itself. For example, excessive howling due to separation anxiety may occur in dogs left alone. In such cases, it's important to understand the cause of the howling and take appropriate measures to help the dog feel safer and more relaxed when left alone.

It's also possible that a dog's howling may be perceived as disruptive in certain environments, such as densely populated residential areas or situations where quiet is required. In such cases, training methods can be employed to control or minimize the howling without suppressing the dog's natural needs and behaviors.

Generally, the goal should not be to indiscriminately minimize a dog's howling, but rather to find a balanced relationship between the dog's natural behavior and the needs of its human companions. This can be achieved through careful observation of the dog, appropriate training, and creating an environment that takes its needs into account.

Triggers:

Loneliness and Separation Anxiety: Dogs are social animals and may howl when they feel abandoned or fearful of being separated from their owners.

Social Communication: Dogs may howl to attract the attention of other dogs or humans in their environment or to announce their presence. This may be part of their instinct to establish contact with other members of their pack.

Response to Specific Sounds: Dogs may respond to loud noises such as sirens, music, or other unusual sounds with howling. These sounds may contain certain frequencies that appeal to dogs' natural instincts and prompt them to howl.

Emotional States: Dogs may howl to express emotions such as fear, pain, frustration, or even joy. Howling can be a way for them to communicate their feelings, especially when they are unable to express them in other ways.

Territorial Behavior: Some dogs may howl to mark their territory or to deter potential intruders. This behavior is more common in territorial dogs or those who feel insecure in a new environment.

Minimizing Howling:

Minimizing howling in dogs requires an under-standing of the underlying causes and a targeted approach aimed at fulfilling the dog's needs and positively influencing its behavior.

Observe your dog's behavior closely and try to determine the situations in which it howls. Is it primarily when it's left alone? Does it react to specific noises? There may also be emotional triggers influencing its howling.

If your dog suffers from separation anxiety and howls when left alone, it's important to help it feel safer when alone. Training and desensitization can help with this. Slow and gradual training, where the dog learns to be alone for short periods and associates positive experiences with it, can help reduce separation anxiety.

An active and fulfilled life can also help minimize a dog's howling. Ensure your dog gets enough exercise, mental stimulation, and social interaction. Regular walks, playtimes, and training sessions can help reduce boredom and loneliness, which can sometimes lead to howling.

Sometimes, simple adjustments in the environment can help minimize a dog's howling. For example, you can use background noise like soft music or a fan to drown out unusual sounds that might prompt the dog to howl. A comfortable sleeping area in a quiet part of the house can also help your dog feel safe and relaxed.

Reward quiet behavior and ignore howling when it's not caused by an urgent need. Use positive reinforcement to teach your dog alternative behaviors associated with rewards. When your dog learns that quiet behavior is rewarded, it's more likely to repeat that behavior.

In more severe cases of excessive howling or separation anxiety, the assistance of a professional dog trainer or behavior specialist may be helpful. They can conduct an individual assessment and develop a training plan tailored to your dog's specific needs.

It's important to note that minimizing a dog's howling does not mean suppressing or preventing its natural behavior. Rather, the goal is to create a balanced environment where the dog feels safe and comfortable and can appropriately control its behavior.

Can Dogs Be Trained to Howl on Command?

Yes, it is possible to train dogs to respond to specific cues or commands that prompt them to howl. However, this requires patience, consistency, and positive reinforcement during training. The key often lies in associating howling with pleasant experiences for the dog. For example, some owners use musical instruments like harmonicas or special howling cues to encourage their dogs to howl. Others use specific words or hand signals as a cue for howling. However, not all dogs are equally receptive to this training, as the willingness to howl heavily depends on the individual personality and temperament of the dog.

Fleeing

Dogs may flee because they feel threatened or fearful. Loud noises such as fireworks or thunderstorms can trigger panic and cause a dog to attempt to escape the noise. Similarly, unfamiliar situations or environments can cause fear, especially if the dog is not adequately accustomed to them.

Boxers may try to escape or flee if they feel threatened, anxious, or if they have not been properly trained to stay within boundaries.

A lack of training or socialization can also lead to dogs fleeing. If a dog has not learned to obey commands or feel secure in different environments, it may feel stressed and try to escape when it feels threatened or uncomfortable.

Some dogs also flee to follow their natural instinct to hunt or explore. Even well-trained dogs may succumb to their hunting instinct in some situations, especially when they encounter potential prey. In such cases, an area that was thought to be secure for the dog may suddenly seem uninteresting, and it may try to escape to pursue its hunting passion.

Understanding the reasons for fleeing behavior is important to take appropriate measures. This may include providing a safe and comfortable home, appropriate training and socialization for the dog, and using safety measures such as fences or leashes to prevent the dog from escaping unsupervised and potentially getting into danger.

Triggers:

Dogs may flee when suddenly exposed to loud noises, such as fireworks, thunderstorms, or loud traffic noise. These loud noises can trigger panic and activate the dog's flight instinct as it tries to escape the noise and seek refuge in a safer place.

Unknown environments or new places can also trigger fleeing behavior. When a dog is brought into a new environment that it is not familiar with or finds intimidating, it may attempt to flee to return to a familiar place or find an environment it perceives as safe.

Anxiety-inducing situations such as confrontations with aggressive animals or people can cause a dog to try to flee to protect itself from a potential threat. In such situations, the dog may instinctively seek an escape route to reach safety.

The feeling of being confined or having insufficient freedom of movement can also trigger fleeing behavior. If a dog feels confined or restricted, it may try to escape to gain more freedom and feel better.

Inadequate socialization or training can also lead to dogs fleeing. A dog that has not been properly socialized or trained may feel insecure and not know how to respond appropriately in stressful situations. In such cases, fleeing behavior could be a reaction to perceived threat or insecurity.

The instinct to hunt can also be a trigger for fleeing behavior. If a dog suddenly encounters potential prey or wildlife, it may follow its natural instinct to hunt or explore, which could lead to it running away from its owner.

Separation anxiety is another potential trigger for fleeing behavior. A dog that is separated from its owners or feels abandoned may try to flee to find its owners or rejoin them.

Hormonal changes, such as during mating season in intact dogs, can also trigger fleeing behavior. During such times, dogs may be more impulsive and less responsive to commands, which could lead to them attempting to escape to fulfill their reproductive drive.

Stress from changes in family dynamics, such as moving or introducing new pets, can also cause dogs to flee. In such situations, dogs may feel insecure or anxious and try to flee to escape the stressful environment.

The attraction of familiar places or individuals outside the home can also trigger fleeing behavior. If a dog feels drawn to a particular place or person, it may try to flee to reach them, especially if it is unsecured and has the opportunity to escape.

These various triggers for fleeing behavior can occur individually or in combination and are important to consider in order to better understand dogs' behavior and take appropriate measures to ensure their safety.

Minimizing Fleeing:

- A well-trained and socialized dog is less susceptible to fleeing behavior. Through training, you can teach your dog important commands such as "Come here" or "Stay," which can be useful in situations where he attempts to flee. Socialization also helps your dog feel safer and more confident in different environments.
- Ensure that your home and yard are secure and dog-proof. Regularly check fences and doors for gaps or damage through which your dog could escape. Use additional security measures such as double fencing or escape-proof locks if necessary.
- Make sure your dog wears a visible and updated ID tag and is microchipped. If he does manage to escape, this facilitates his return to you if he is found.
- Be mindful of where your dog is and what might potentially scare or trigger him to flee. Avoid situations that could induce fear, and keep a close eye on your dog, especially in unfamiliar environments or during loud events like fireworks.

- Reduce stress factors in your dog's life by providing a stable and consistent environment. Avoid frequent moves or major household changes that could cause stress and uncertainty.
- Ensure your dog gets enough exercise and mental stimulation to reduce boredom and excess energy. A well-exercised dog is generally less prone to fleeing behavior.
- Reward your dog for good behavior and for remaining calm or following your instructions in challenging situations. Positive reinforcement can help strengthen the bond and trust between you and your dog.

By implementing these measures, you can minimize the risk of fleeing behavior in your dog and provide him with a safe and happy home.

Which technologies and tools are available to track lost dogs?

There are various technologies and tools that can help track lost dogs. GPS trackers, attached to the dog's collar, allow owners to track their dog's exact location via a smartphone app. Microchips are a permanent identification method that enables shelters and veterinarians to scan lost dogs and identify their owners. Additionally, there are specialized search dog teams trained to track lost pets, as well as online platforms and apps where owners can post photos and information about their missing dogs to enlist the public's help in the search.

Housetraining

House training in dogs is a crucial process aimed at teaching the dog to relieve itself outside and keep the inside of the house clean. This process requires time, patience, and consistency from the dog owner.

The first step in house training is to teach the dog that the house is not an appropriate place for its needs. This is often accompanied by the use of specific signals, such as a particular word or gesture, to show the dog that it's time to go outside. A regular routine for outdoor trips helps the dog learn when it has the opportunity to relieve itself.

It's important to reward the dog for the right behavior. Once the dog has relieved itself outside, it should be praised enthusiastically and perhaps even rewarded with a treat. Positive reinforcement is a key element of house training, as it teaches the dog that relieving itself outside is a good thing.

However, it's also important to note that punishments for accidents in the house are not effective. If the dog does something wrong in the house, it's best to remain calm and thoroughly clean the accident to remove any odors that might encourage the dog to urinate or defecate in the same spot again.

Patience is the key to success in house training. Every dog learns at its own pace, and it may take some time for it to be fully house trained. However, consistency in the routine and in praising the right behavior will help ensure that the process is successful.

Step by Step Introduction:

- Establish fixed times for meals, water intake, and outdoor trips. A puppy should go outside approximately every two hours, as well as after waking up, playing, and eating.
- Designate a specific area outdoors for the dog to do its business. Always take the dog to the same spot to teach it where to relieve itself.
- Watch for signs that the dog needs to do its business, such as sniffing around, circling, or restlessness. If you notice such signs, take the dog outside immediately.
- Once the dog has done its business outside, praise it enthusiastically and give it a reward, such as a treat or praise. This reinforces the behavior and encourages the dog to do it again.
- If the dog has an accident in the house, remain calm and clean the area thoroughly to remove odors. Punishments can unsettle the dog and make the house training process more difficult.
- House training takes time and consistency. Be patient and remain consistent in your training. Every dog learns at its own pace.
- Keep the dog closely monitored in the initial stages of training or limit its access to other areas of the house to prevent accidents. A crate or puppy playpen can be helpful for confining the dog when you are not nearby to supervise.

What common mistakes do dog owners make during house training?

Another mistake is punishing the dog after an accident. Punishment can lead to fear or insecurity in the dog and even make house training more difficult. Finally, inadequate cleaning of accident sites is a mistake. If the smell of urine or feces remains in the house, the dog is more likely to be encouraged to use the same spot again.

How long does it typically take for a puppy to be house trained?

On average, it can take between four and six months for a puppy to be fully house trained. Some may learn faster, while others may take more time. It depends on various factors such as the breed of the dog, its personality, and its environment.

What role do feeding times play in a dog's house training?

Feeding times play an important role in a dog's house training as they can help regulate its bowel movements. Regular feeding at the same time every day can also help predict when the dog is likely to need to do its business. Consistent feeding times help stabilize the dog's metabolism and regulate its need for going to the toilet.

Barking

Barking in dogs is a fascinating behavior pattern that can have various meanings and causes. It is a form of communication that occurs between dogs and also between dogs and humans. This behavior is often complex and can be influenced by various factors.

Boxers are known for their vocalizations and may bark to communicate various needs or alert their owners to perceived threats.

One reason why dogs bark lies in their nature as social animals. Through barking, they can convey various messages to other dogs or even humans. For example, they may express their joy or excitement through loud barking when they see a familiar person or when they look forward to an upcoming play session. On the other hand, dogs may also bark out of fear or uncertainty to communicate their discomfort or concerns. A dog feeling threatened may exhibit aggressive barking to warn or drive away potential intruders.

Another reason for dogs barking often lies in their territorial instinct. Dogs have an innate need to defend their territory, whether it's their home, their territory in the park, or even their favorite spot on the sofa. If they feel their territory is threatened, whether by other dogs, animals, or even unfamiliar humans, they may bark loudly to mark their presence and deter potential intruders. For example, a dog may bark along a fence if it notices other dogs nearby to show that the area is already claimed.

Furthermore, dogs may bark for various other reasons, such as to attract attention or to combat boredom or loneliness. If a dog feels neglected or has the need to interact with its owner, it may try to gain their attention through barking. This can be particularly common when the dog wants to make a connection, whether it's for a cuddle session, a play session, or even for a walk.

It's important to understand that barking is a natural part of dog behavior and that there can be various reasons for it. By attentively observing the dog's body language and situation, one can often better understand why it's barking and respond appropriately. Training and positive reinforcement can help reduce unwanted barking and promote better communication between humans and dogs.

Minimizing Barking:

Identify and understand causes: Excessive barking can have various causes, including fear, boredom, territorial behavior, seeking attention, or pain. It's important to identify the specific triggers of your dog's barking to find effective solutions. This requires thorough observation of your dog's behavior in different situations.

Training and obedience: A well-trained dog is less prone to excessive barking. Structured training based on positive reinforcement can help your dog learn basic obedience commands and control its behavior. Through regular training, you can also teach your dog alternative behaviors to exhibit instead of barking.

Distraction and engagement: Dogs sometimes bark out of boredom or understimulation. Provide sufficient physical and mental stimulation to fulfill your dog's needs. Walks, interactive games, intellectually challenging toys, and training sessions can help channel your dog's energy and satisfy its need for stimulation.

Desensitization and counterconditioning: If your dog reacts to certain stimuli or situations with excessive barking, desensitization and counterconditioning can help.

This involves gradual exposure to the stimulus in controlled situations to reduce your dog's response. Combine this with positive reinforcement to reward good behavior and minimize barking.

Ignoring the unwanted behavior: In some cases, ignoring excessive barking can help reduce it. For example, if your dog barks for attention, try ignoring it until it's quiet, then reward it for calm behavior. This teaches your dog that unwanted barking is not rewarded, while calm behavior is positively reinforced.

Professional help: For persistent or hard-to-control barking, it may be advisable to seek professional help from a dog trainer or behavior specialist. They can provide an individual assessment of your dog's behavior and give you specific tips and techniques to effectively reduce barking.

What role does the temperament of the dog play in barking?

The temperament of the dog plays an important role. A confident and dominant dog may be inclined to bark more to demonstrate its strength or territoriality, while a shy or fearful dog may bark more out of insecurity. The dog's personality, experiences, and learning history can also influence its barking. For instance, a dog with a strong protector instinct may tend to bark more to defend its territory or alert to potential threats.

Professionals

Whether you've just welcomed a new furry friend into your home or you're thinking about it, understanding the importance of puppy classes, dog schools, and professional trainers is crucial for setting your puppy up for success.

Puppy Class

A puppy class tailored for Boxers marks a pivotal stage in the early development of our furry companions, offering a wealth of advantages. Geared towards puppies aged approximately 8 to 16 weeks, this specialized program aims to instill fundamental skills and behaviors, laying the groundwork for a well-mannered and socially adept adult dog.

Within the confines of a puppy class, young Boxers have the invaluable opportunity to cultivate crucial social aptitudes. Through supervised interactions with fellow canines, they learn to navigate appropriate play dynamics and acclimate to the presence of other animals. For instance, a pup accustomed to solitary play at home may acquire the art of engaging with peers without being overly rough or timid.

Moreover, fundamental obedience commands take center stage in the curriculum, serving as keystones for effective training. Puppies grasp the essentials of commands like "sit," "down," and "come," fostering clearer communication between owner and dog. Consider a scenario where a Boxer pup, prone to leash pulling, learns to walk serenely by their owner's side through structured training in the puppy class.

Housebreaking, a perennial challenge for many dog owners, receives due attention in the puppy class setting.

Here, novices can glean insights and strategies from seasoned trainers on guiding their pups to discern appropriate times and places for relieving themselves.

Beyond the realm of practical instruction, participation in a puppy class nurtures a deeper bond between Boxer and owner. Through shared learning and collaborative training sessions, they forge a robust connection that underpins a thriving partnership. Such cohesion proves invaluable when confronting potential behavioral issues, such as excessive vocalization or destructive tendencies.

Dog School

A dog school serves as a hub offering a diverse array of services geared towards the training, care, and overall well-being of dogs and their owners. These establishments not only provide foundational obedience courses but also specialize in tailored programs to address the unique requirements of various canine companions.

While both a dog school and a puppy class extend support to dog owners in nurturing their pets' training and welfare, there are distinctions between the two. Whereas a puppy class is tailored for pups aged roughly 8 to 16 weeks, a dog school accommodates dogs of all ages and stages of development. The focal point of a puppy class revolves around instilling fundamental skills and behaviors crucial for early life stages, whereas a dog school offers a broader spectrum of services catered to canines at different life stages.

In a puppy class, the spotlight often shines on socialization, basic obedience, and house training. Conversely, a dog school may broaden its offerings to encompass specialized programs such as behavior counseling, agility courses, and therapy dog training.

Another disparity lies in the format of instruction. Puppy classes typically operate as condensed courses honing in on the specific needs of young dogs, while training at a dog school tends to unfold as continuous and ongoing support to nurture a dog's development across an extended duration.

Professional Trainer

If you're grappling with behavioral challenges in your Boxer or struggling to meet your training objectives independently, enlisting the expertise of a professional dog trainer can be a wise step forward. This decision holds merit across a spectrum of scenarios.

When confronted with issues like aggression, incessant barking, or persistent leash pulling, a seasoned trainer can offer invaluable insights into root causes and devise effective strategies for resolution. Armed with years of experience and specialized knowledge, a trainer can introduce novel training techniques and enhance your understanding of your Boxer's behavior, facilitating clearer communication between you and your canine companion.

Even if progress appears elusive or setbacks arise despite consistent efforts, the intervention of a trainer can catalyze significant breakthroughs. By pinpointing potential pitfalls and fine-tuning training approaches, they can steer your efforts towards greater efficacy.

For those uncertain about where to begin or which methods align best with their Boxer's temperament, a professional trainer serves as a guiding beacon. They can craft a bespoke training regimen tailored to your Boxer's unique needs and capabilities, setting you both on a path to success.

Moreover, should you aspire to prepare your Boxer for specific roles or scenarios—be it therapy dog duties, search and rescue missions, or competitive endeavors like agility—a trainer can furnish you with the requisite expertise and resources. Through targeted training sessions, you and your Boxer can hone the skills essential for excelling in your chosen pursuits.

Life changes such as relocation or the arrival of a new family member can impact your Boxer's behavior. In such transitions, a professional trainer can offer invaluable support, guiding you through the process of acclimating your Boxer to the altered circumstances and fostering a stronger bond between you both.

At the End, remember that it's just the beginning of a broader exploration.

We hope you are happy with this book.

The satisfaction of our readers is our priority and we would be happy if you could give us your feedback on the book.

It would therefore be great if you would take a moment to write a customer review on Amazon. It only takes you a few seconds.

By doing this, you will help other readers on Amazon make better purchasing decisions.

Thank you!

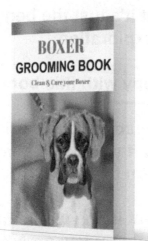
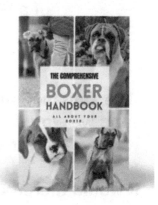

Boxer Grooming Book

$29,99

Purchase on Amazon

Boxer Handbook

$49,99

Purchase on Amazon

SCAN ME

Made in United States
North Haven, CT
25 November 2024

60926150R00098